The Imaginary Present

POETS ON POETRY

Derek Pollard, Series Editor
Donald Hall, Founding Editor

TITLES IN THE SERIES
Amy Catanzano, *The Imaginary Present*
Khadijah Queen, *Radical Poetics*
Nathaniel Perry, *Joy (or Something Darker, but Like It)*
Dan Beachy-Quick, *How to Draw a Circle*
Christina Pugh, *Ghosts and the Overplus*
Norman Finkelstein, *To Go Into the Words*
Major Jackson, *A Beat Beyond*, edited by Amor Kohli
Jane Miller, *From the Valley of Bronze Camels*
Tony Hoagland, *The Underground Poetry Metro Transportation System for Souls*
Philip Metres, *The Sound of Listening*
Julie Carr, *Someone Shot My Book*
Claudia Keelan, *Ecstatic Émigré*
Rigoberto Gonzalez, *Pivotal Voices, Era of Transition*
Garrett Hongo, *The Mirror Diary*
Marianne Boruch, *The Little Death of Self*
Yusef Komunyakaa, *Condition Red*
Khaled Mattawa, *How Long Have You Been With Us?*
Aaron Shurin, *The Skin of Meaning*

ALSO AVAILABLE, BOOKS BY
Elizabeth Alexander, Meena Alexander, Kazim Ali, A. R. Ammons, John Ashbery, David Baker, Robert Bly, Bruce Bond, Philip Booth, Marianne Boruch, Hayden Carruth, Amy Clampitt, Alfred Corn, Douglas Crase, Robert Creeley, Donald Davie, Thomas M. Disch, Ed Dorn, Martín Espada, Annie Finch, Tess Gallagher, Sandra M. Gilbert, Dana Gioia, Linda Gregerson, Allen Grossman, Thom Gunn, Marilyn Hacker, Rachel Hadas, John Haines, Donald Hall, Joy Harjo, Robert Hayden, Edward Hirsch, Daniel Hoffman, Jonathan Holden, John Hollander, Paul Hoover, Andrew Hudgins, T. R. Hummer, Laura (Riding) Jackson, Josephine Jacobsen, Mark Jarman, Lawrence Joseph, Galway Kinnell, Kenneth Koch, John Koethe, Yusef Komunyakaa, Marilyn Krysl, Maxine Kumin, Martin Lammon (editor), Philip Larkin, David Lehman, Philip Levine, Larry Levis, John Logan, William Logan, David Mason, William Matthews, Joyelle McSweeney, William Meredith, Jane Miller, David Mura, Carol Muske, Alice Notley, Geoffrey O'Brien, Gregory Orr, Alicia Suskin Ostriker, Ron Padgett, Marge Piercy, Grace Schulman, Anne Sexton, Karl Shapiro, Reginald Shepherd, Charles Simic, William Stafford, Anne Stevenson, Cole Swenson, May Swenson, James Tate, Richard Tillinghast, C. K. Williams, Alan Williamson, David Wojahn, Charles Wright, James Wright, John Yau, and Stephen Yenser

For a complete list of titles, please see www.press.umich.edu

The Imaginary Present

Essays in Quantum Poetics

AMY CATANZANO

University of Michigan Press
Ann Arbor

Copyright © 2025 by Amy Catanzano
All rights reserved

For questions or permissions, please contact um.press.perms@umich.edu

Published in the United States of America by the
University of Michigan Press
Manufactured in the United States of America
Printed on acid-free paper
First published February 2025
A CIP catalog record for this book is available from the British Library.

Library of Congress Cataloging-in-Publication data has been applied for.

ISBN 978-0-472-03983-8 (paper : alk. paper)

ISBN 978-0-472-22209-4 (e-book)

Acknowledgments

Although the essay-poems in this book are linked chapters about the relationship between literature and physics, many began as distinct pieces responding to my site visits and residencies at scientific research centers, talks at academic and scientific institutions, and invitations by editors of print and online journals. My deepest thanks to the individuals and organizations that provided me opportunities to develop this work.

A number of the chapters have been supported by my three visits to the European Organization for Nuclear Research, known as CERN, in Meyrin, Switzerland. My first visit (2016) was funded by Wake Forest University in Winston-Salem, North Carolina, where I teach, through a W. C. Archie Endowed Fund for Faculty Excellence Award. That visit was sponsored by astroparticle physicist and poet Juan José Gómez Cadenas. My second visit (2019) was sponsored by Arts at CERN and funded by the A Toroidal LHC Apparatus (ATLAS) experiment at the Large Hadron Collider (LHC) and its US ATLAS Outreach initiative, headed at the time by particle physicist Mark C. Kruse. My third visit (2023) was funded also by ATLAS and sponsored by the US Department of Energy's Brookhaven National Laboratory. These visits included research on particle physics, poetry projects, touring experiments, and speaking with physicists and staff, including James Beacham, Sarah Charley, Michael Doser, Luis Álvarez-Gaumé, Fabiola Gianotti, Gian Francesco Giudice, Steve Goldfarb, Markus Nordberg, Kate Pachal, and João Pequenão. Thank you to each of them, my sponsors, and CERN. I'm especially grateful to physicist, science storyteller, and filmmaker James Beacham, with whom I've been collaborating on an idea for a poetry-physics experiment.

Some of this material is inspired by my attendance at a 2016 scientific review of the NEXT neutrino experiment at the Canfranc Underground Laboratory (LSC) in Canfranc, Spain, where I was funded by Wake Forest

vi | *Acknowledgments*

also through a W. C. Archie Endowed Fund for Faculty Excellence Award as well as LSC. Thank you to Juan José Gómez Cadenas for the invitation. I'm grateful to him for connecting me to the Mestizajes Programme on the intersections of art, science, and literature at the Donostia International Physics Center in San Sebastián, Spain, where I was invited to give a talk on quantum poetics in 2016. Thank you to physicist and writer Gustavo A. Schwartz, who directs the Mestizajes Programme, and literary scholar Víctor Bermúdez for our conversations there and inviting me to contribute to their edited collection, *#Nodos: Entangling Sciences and Humanities*, published in Spanish (2017) by Next Door Publishers and English (2019) by Intellect Press. I also wish to thank poet Rae Armantrout for introducing me to Juan José Gómez Cadenas.

"The Poetics of Scale" draws from my site visit in 2018 to the Cerro Tololo Inter-American Observatory, overseen by the US National Science Foundation's NOIRLab, in the Chilean Andes. Funded by Wake Forest again through a W. C. Archie Endowed Fund for Faculty Excellence Award, I was sponsored by the observatory's Broadening Horizons program. My work involved conducting research on the Dark Energy Survey and participating in overnight observations of deep space with astrophysicists in the control room of the Víctor M. Blanco Telescope. Thank you to astrophysicist Joshua A. Frieman, former director of the Dark Energy Survey, for our conversations at Cerro Tololo and welcoming me into his work, and transmedia artist Lynn Book for introducing me to Josh. Thank you as well to astrophysicist Satya Gontcho A Gontcho for our friendship at Cerro Tololo and subsequent collaborations; astronomer Stephen Heathcote, director of the observatory at the time; and engineer Javier Rojas and science operations specialist Alysha Shugart for coordinating my talks at Cerro Tololo and La Serena.

"Poetry in Superposition" first appeared in the journal of political thought and philosophy *Crisis and Critique*: "The Present of Poetry" (2022), published by the Dialectical Materialism Collective and edited by philosophers Agon Hamza and Frank Ruda. Thank you to them for inviting me to be part of this issue.

"The Positron Passport" first appeared in somewhat different form in *CounterText: A Journal for the Study of the Post-Literary*: "Poetry Elsewhere, Elsewhere Poetry" (2021), published by Edinburgh University Press and guest edited by literary scholar Ming-Qian Ma. I'm grateful to Ma for his longtime support of my work and the invitation to be part of this issue.

Some of the chapters in this book were first published, in 2009–2012 and 2020, and in somewhat different form, by poet Jerome Rothenberg in *Poems and Poetics*, later distributed by the online journal *Jacket2*, associated with PennSound and the Kelly Writers House at the University of Pennsylvania. Thank you to him for his early and ongoing support.

"Physics of the Impossible" and "U+F+O+L+A+N+G+U+A+G+E," in somewhat different form, first appeared in my commentary series on quantum poetics for *Jacket2* in 2015. Thank you to publisher Al Filreis and editors Jessica Lowenthal and Michael S. Hennessey.

"Spin the Kaleidoscope" draws from my participation in a video project by artist and filmmaker David Blair, *The Telepathic Motion Picture of THE LOST TRIBES*, a serialized sequel to his cult classic film *Wax or the Discovery of Television Among the Bees* (1991). My participation in the video project was filmed at the Robert C. Byrd Green Bank Telescope in West Virginia. A portion of the footage was included in David's solo-show video installation at Galerie de l'Angle in Paris in 2017. Thank you to him.

Some of the material in this book comes from a response that I provided to literary scholar and poet Katie L. Price for her commentary series for *Jacket2* in 2015. An excerpt of my response was reprinted in the commentaries section of Jerome Rothenberg's edited anthology *Technicians of the Sacred: A Range of Poetries from Africa, America, Asia, Europe, and Oceania*, third edition, revised and expanded (University of California Press, 2017). My thanks to them.

A portion of the introduction appeared in a 2022 opinion-editorial that I was invited to write for the American Physical Society's *Physics* magazine. My poem in "The Imaginary Present" first appeared in 2013 in the literary journal *Washington Square Review*, published by New York University. "The Poetry Accelerator," in somewhat different form, first appeared in 2010 in *Critiphoria: A Journal of Poetry and Criticism*. Thank you to the publishers and editors.

I wish to thank my friends and colleagues at Wake Forest in the Department of English, Charlotte and Philip Hanes Art Gallery, and Department of Art for their support, including artist and arts curator Paul Bright, artist Leigh Ann Hallberg, fiction writer Joanna Ruocco, and literary scholar viii | *Acknowledgments*

Judith Madera. Thank you to the university for my funding, research leaves, and a summer research award that supported this book. I'm thankful as well to Wake Forest's Department of Physics for inviting me to participate in their colloquium series to give a talk on quantum poetics in 2014. I'm grateful to Wake Forest physics faculty members Paul Anderson, Eric Carlson, and Daniel Kim-Shapiro for guest teaching in my creative writing course on physics and poetry in 2022 and meeting with me to discuss physics. Thank you to literary scholar Dean Franco, The Humanities Institute at Wake Forest, and Reynolda House Museum of American Art for awarding me funding to convene *Entanglements: A Conference on the Intersections of Poetry, Science, and the Arts* at Wake Forest in 2019. I also wish to thank my friends and former colleagues at the Jack Kerouac School of Disembodied Poetics at Naropa University in Boulder, Colorado, for their early encouragement of this work, especially poet Reed Bye, fiction writer Junior Burke, writer Bhanu Kapil, and poet Anne Waldman.

Thank you to theoretical physicist Luis Álvarez-Gaumé and artist and arts curator Lorraine Walsh, as well as visiting theoretical physicist Giuseppe Mussardo, at the Simons Center for Geometry and Physics at Stony Brook University in New York, where I wrote and first presented on *World Lines: A Quantum Supercomputer Poem* (2018–present) while serving as the inaugural poet-in-residence in the Art & Culture initiative. Thank you to climate scientist and mathematician Michael Taylor for our current collaboration involving *World Lines*.

I'm deeply grateful to the University of Michigan Press, including Poets on Poetry series editor Derek Pollard, associate editor Haley Winkle, and managing editor Marcia LaBrenz for supporting this book and steering it through to publication. I'm also grateful to the copy editor, Akiko Yamagata of Graphite Editing, for her exceptional editing of the manuscript.

My vision for this book grew alongside the friendship and fellowship of other poets and fellow travelers, especially Will Alexander, Rae Armantrout, Adam Dickinson, Andrew Joron, Rodrigo Toscano, and Anne Waldman. My warmest thanks to each of them.

Lastly, thank you to my family for their love and support, especially Attilio and Cathy Catanzano for our rich conversations about the ideas in this book and their unwavering encouragement, and to my dear friends Matthew Baird, Lynn Book, and Chelsey Minnis.

Contents

Time Is Not an Arrow: An Introduction to Quantum Poetics	1
Writing the Speed of Light	12
The Multiverse	18
The New Spacetime	22
'Pataphysics Is an Iridescent Veil	25
Third Mind	31
The Imaginary Present	34
The Reader as a Quantum Observer	38
Physics of the Impossible	39
The Poetry Accelerator	42
The Poetics of Scale	44
Just Schrödinger the Text!	47
Poetry and Science: The Two Most Incompatible Disciplines	51
Spin the Kaleidoscope	54
Poetry and the Fourth Dimension	56
The People of the Fifth Dimension	59
The Positron Passport	61
To Be in Any Form	83

x | *Contents*

The Password to the Quantum Supercomputer Poem
Will Be NCC-1701   84

The Violet Doorway   85

Poetry in Superposition   89

U+F+O+L+A+N+G+U+A+G+E   91

The Subtle Web of Thought   94

Metaphor and Decay   97

The Origami Time Machine   98

The Physics of Existence   99

The Matrix   105

Notes   109

Forever—is composed of Nows—
EMILY DICKINSON

Time Is Not an Arrow

An Introduction to Quantum Poetics

One doesn't need to be a poet or scientist to get the sense that time is not what it appears to be. While some societies see time as linear with a past, present, and future, others see it as cyclical or abstract. We know that calendars, while useful in organizing time, are influenced by cultural ideas about nature. For example, a solar year in the Western Gregorian calendar is based on the number of revolutions that the Earth takes around the Sun in a twelve-month period. A lunisolar year in the Eastern Chinese calendar is based on astronomical observations of the Sun's longitude and the Moon's phases. Our experience of time is linked to memory and perception, shaped by our neurobiology and psychological landscapes. Discussions of time have featured prominently in philosophy and beyond.

When we look at how physics treats time, especially over the past hundred years, we see that scientists have made groundbreaking discoveries about this mysterious phenomenon. Physics is the branch of the natural sciences that describes the structure of matter and how the fundamental parts of the universe interact. While physicists have achieved knowledge about time that exceeds our ordinary assumptions, so far this knowledge has yet to fully make its way into our everyday understanding. It turns out, for example, that time cannot be separated from space. From the quantum world within atoms to the cosmological world of outer space, spacetime operates in extraordinary ways that have profound implications on reality.

As a poet who is always striving to maximize the artistry of my poetry, I began noticing how literary devices such as line breaks and rhythm uniquely navigate time and space. I started to see the page itself as a field of spacetime, one that was interacting with poetic language. A poem's ideas, or what I think of as the "mind" of a poem, and a poem's form, or what I think of as the "body" of a poem, can slow or quicken a reader's sense of time through their interaction. Some poems even seem to suspend time. It was my curiosity about how artistic language works with spacetime that led me to study physics in addition to literature, writing, and philosophy. As my poetry practice developed, I saw that the radical permissiveness of poetry gives it both power and intensity, since we use language to think and create. I also continued to prize innovation in poetry, since it was leading me to write—and live life—with greater depth.

It was about seven years after graduate school at the Iowa Writers' Workshop, while I was teaching at Naropa University, that my curiosity about time sparked my study of physics. I read books on physics and learned how assumptions about time, space, and matter were challenged in relativity and quantum theory. I started to apply what I was learning in theoretical physics to my writing, developing poems influenced by physics and essays about poetry in relation to scientific inquiry. I focused on quantum theory, which is often viewed as counterintuitive by scientists and nonscientists alike. As a poet trained in unconventional thinking, some of the conceptual complexities of quantum theory were surprisingly lucid to me, and so I began calling this new practice "quantum poetics." While I was hesitant to brand what I was doing with a single term, I found it useful in situating my ideas.

About ten years later, with access to university research funding in a new teaching position at Wake Forest University, I began going on site visits to scientific research centers, where I developed my knowledge of physics by talking with scientists and touring experiments. I soon received invitations and funding from scientific research centers for longer visits and residencies. Now, in addition to my individual projects, I collaborate with scientists and give talks and poetry readings at scientific institutions. My knowledge of physics has evolved alongside my experience with poetry, leading me to new questions about what is possible when these fields are explored together.

Quantum poetics begins with the notion that ordinary conceptions of time, space, and matter must be changed to account for cutting-edge scientific knowledge and poetic practice. To achieve this goal, I treat the literary arts as a physics, and physics as an artform. This approach departs from the usual placement of literature solely within literary, artistic,

Time Is Not an Arrow | 3

political, and cultural studies, as well as the usual placement of physics solely within the natural sciences. In quantum poetics, I apply scientific knowledge to the practice of poetry and use poetics, the frameworks that help us critically read literature, to interpret this knowledge.

After seventeen years of studying physics as a poet, I now see the field as not only a branch of the natural sciences but also a philosophical discourse that is subject to the artistic paradigms produced by its own scientific theories and experiments. I also see poetry outside of common attitudes where it is viewed strictly as an expression of the sublime or a cultural and personal utility. Allied with the serious play and subversive thinking of writer Alfred Jarry and his "science of imaginary solutions," known as 'pataphysics, quantum poetics investigates our open questions about the material universe. Joining the imagination with rationality, quantum poetics seeks "solutions" to these open questions while rejecting the intellectual vagueness and controlling dogma associated with religion and metaphysics.

Quantum poetics works to expand what constitutes literary art and physics. The relationship of quantum phenomena to the study and practice of poetry that I discuss in this book challenges how literary art and physics are defined, why they are valued, the forms they can take, and the contexts they can engage. As a result, quantum poetics aims to dissolve not only the constructed boundaries between the literary and the scientific but also the creative and the critical. The traditional split we often see between scholars and poets is not so unlike the split that occurred at the turn of the twentieth century between theoretical physicists, who use theories in physics for developing models of our universe, and experimental physicists, who conduct experiments. Unlike some poet-critics, who write separate works of poetry and literary criticism, my poetics often combines prose with poetry. This book, for example, is structured by linked chapters that move across genres and performance zones, including literary and scientific analysis, my own poetry, theory, lyric essay, memoir, and speculative nonfiction.

Based on the idea that exploring discoveries in physics is necessary to treating language as a complex system within literature that aims to be innovative, quantum poetics is committed to pushing past the margins of normative logic. As mathematician Shing-Tung Yau and science writer Steve Nadis say in *The Shape of Inner Space: String Theory and the*

4 | THE IMAGINARY PRESENT

Geometry of the Universe's Hidden Dimensions (2012), "In contemplating higher-dimensional spaces, we must allow for movements in directions we can't readily imagine. We're not talking about heading somewhere in between north and west like northwest or even 'North by Northwest.' We're talking about heading off the grid altogether, following arrows in a coordinate system that has yet to be drawn."[1] Even though quantum poetics exists within a long tradition of writers responding to science, it departs from some of the conventions of this tradition by "heading off the grid altogether" in treating poetry and physics in union.

While the term quantum poetics has been used by writers and thinkers such as Daniel Albright to discuss modernist poets, Stephanie Strickland to discuss electronic poetry, and Gwyneth Lewis to discuss poetic form, what distinguishes my use of the phrase is the central role that quantum theory plays in my practice. Though the notion of the quantum is now common in literary fiction and across the arts, quantum poetics uniquely explores the principles of physics through poetry, and poetry through those principles. I'm especially excited by quantum computing, particle physics, and astrophysics. My interest in these areas of scientific research has brought me to the European Organization for Nuclear Research, known as CERN, in Switzerland; the Cerro Tololo Inter-American Observatory in Chile; the Simons Center for Geometry and Physics at Stony Brook University in New York; and elsewhere.

At CERN, I'm working with particle physicist James Beacham to encode a cowritten poem into a particle accelerator like the Large Hadron Collider (LHC), which searches for new forms of matter in a seventeen-mile tunnel underground by colliding subatomic particles at high speeds. Once our particle-poem is collided, we'll invite others to make additional poems from the data sets resulting from the collision. We've cowritten a scientific paper outlining the technical specifications of the experiment, which we're submitting to journals. We're also writing a book, a *User Manual*, for future generations to collide poems in more advanced particle colliders, including one that could potentially access the Planck scale. If physicists can find a way to access the Planck scale, which refers to the limits of the known laws of physics, all of their questions about the universe will be answered and new questions will arise.

I first met James during my second visit to CERN, when I worked with the LHC's A Toroidal LHC Apparatus experiment, known as ATLAS. I was brought to CERN by particle physicist Mark C. Kruse. A professor of physics at Duke University, Mark was part of the team that famously discovered the Higgs boson subatomic particle at CERN. That discovery led to the verification of the Higgs field, an invisible field that exists everywhere and with which all matter in the universe must interact to gain mass. James and I continued our collaboration in person at CERN a few years later, when I was funded by ATLAS again and sponsored by the US Department of Energy's Brookhaven National Laboratory.

When James and I met, I joined a small group of visitors accompanied by CERN physicists and staff and went underground to see the LHC while it was temporarily offline. We took pressurized elevators to the ATLAS and Compact Muon Solenoid (CMS) detectors, where the particle collisions that seek out new forms of matter occur. Designed in elaborate layers of wheel-shaped metal overlaid with braided tubes, the detectors look like kaleidoscopic mosaics in motion, a complex interplay of the fluid and the fixed, the artificial and the organic. The center portal of the CMS detector was open because of work being done. I was close enough to the collision chamber that I could see inside. My interest in science had taken me, a poet, directly to where the Higgs boson subatomic particle was discovered and where other new particles of matter could someday emerge.

The next day, James brought me to see new upgrades being built for ATLAS. Named the New Small Wheels, though they are massive, the upgrades look like giant blue flowers woven with mint-green veins under futuristic silver spokes. We spent hours in front of one flower talking about an idea I had, when the LHC launched, to encode a poem inside the protons of a particle collider. The idea was inspired by artist Eduardo Kac's biopoetry and poet Christian Bök's bioart. To my surprise, James said the idea may be technically possible. We immediately began brainstorming the experiment. Under the spell of the blue flowers, and through the fortuitous circumstance of shared vision, our idea grew, as poems do.

Another collaboration of mine involves astrophysicist Satya Gontcho A Gontcho, based at Lawrence Berkeley National Laboratory. We met at the Cerro Tololo Inter-American Observatory when I was conducting research on the Dark Energy Survey, an international collaboration of scientists exploring how dark energy may be responsible for the expansion of the universe. Their research involves creating a high-resolution

6 | THE IMAGINARY PRESENT

map of the universe through imaging with a special camera they built and mounted on a telescope. I participated in overnight observations of deep space with the astrophysicists, seeing far-away galaxies in the control room of the telescope as it imaged them. We also stargazed outside the telescope, since the observatory is a Dark Sky Sanctuary. After my visit, I wrote a book-length poem about dark energy research in relation to art and the cosmology of the Indigenous inhabitants of Cerro Tololo. Satya, who is not only an astrophysicist but also a trained practitioner of a classical Indian dance known as Odissi, choreographed an original dance to a portion of my book, and we performed this danced-poem together. We're now collaborating on another project, drawing from her work in a different scientific collaboration, the Dark Energy Spectroscopic Instrument Survey. Our project involves making an experimental film that explores the poetics of her scientific experiment. My poetry will be the soundtrack, and her dance will accompany other visuals on-screen.

At the Simons Center for Geometry and Physics, I wrote an unusual poem titled *World Lines: A Quantum Supercomputer Poem* (2018), based on a theoretical model of a topological quantum computer. After talking with theoretical physicist Giuseppe Mussardo during an earlier visit to the Simons Center, I learned about topological quantum computing, which computes by quantum knots, and spent the next six months studying it. Quantum computers, still being developed, compute information using quantum bits, known as qubits, instead of digital bits, which allows processing at a speed billions of times faster. My poem replaces the qubits in a theorized model of a topological quantum computer with lines of poetry. Each qubit in the model I used is made of two quasiparticles known as anyons that crisscross or braid over and under one another in clockwise and counterclockwise motions toward a computation. Anyons were first theorized by physicist and Nobel Prize recipient Frank Wilczek.

As anyons braid, they create a physical record or memory of their past trajectories through spacetime. These paths that anyons remember are called world lines by physicists. I was creating the poem on a blackboard in my loaned office at the Simons Center and wrote each line of poetry that corresponds to a world line using either blue- or green-colored chalk to evoke the natural world, inspired by the name of the paths that anyons take. When two lines of my poem braid where anyons would braid, they share a word, written in white chalk that day, where ordinarily a quantum knot would occur in a topological quantum computer.

A reader can read the poem as four couplets that correspond, top to bottom, to the four-qubit model of the topological quantum computer that I was using, or they can choose a branch of poetry to follow when they get to a shared word. As a result of the poem's form, there are multiple poems within the poem in what's known as quantum superposition, where, according to the Copenhagen interpretation of quantum theory, the quantum states of subatomic particles are at once in all points in spacetime until coming into a defined state of existence after being observed or measured. Quantum superposition is a key element of quantum theory and quantum computers. Whereas a digital bit can exist only as a one or zero, a qubit can exist as a one, a zero, or any quantum superposition of one and zero.

When I wrote *World Lines*, I knew there were multiple poems within it because of the choices that readers would make as they followed my world lines, but I didn't know how to calculate how many. Michael Taylor, a climate researcher and mathematician based at the University of East Anglia in the UK, knew how to make such a calculation. He created an artificial intelligence program using a quantum script that he wrote to read my poem and express all possible versions. After parsing each sentence in the poem and identifying branch points—the shared words—he trained a linguistic processor to choose world lines that are semantically logical to track how different topological paths move through a text map into different versions of the poem. While the project is in progress, so far the artificial intelligence has read over a thousand variant poems within the original poem. I'm using the variants for a collection of computational poetry, where I will present the original poem, the version of the poem that appears as four couplets, the first ninety-six variants that the artificial intelligence read, and textual experiments that I'm performing on each variant. A few years after I wrote *World Lines*, anyons were engineered for the first time by physicists using quantum processors.[2]

Collaborations like these ones help break down disciplinary silos that have existed for over a century and diversify thinking and methodologies. They also can protect science from destructive commercial and military aims through social critiques that are common in the arts.

8 | THE IMAGINARY PRESENT

My approach to quantum poetics contains an intellectual commitment to try and accurately represent the science I engage. Since my readership includes enthusiasts of both poetry and science, I work to provide accessible information on literature, art, and physics in this book, which may appear common to experts but is necessary to those who are not.

While this book is largely singular in drawing from a poet's practice of working in particle physics laboratories and astronomical observatories, it participates in a growing trend where the literary arts are conducted across disciplines. The ideas here also are participating in a momentous cultural shift in science, where the scope of scientific practice is including more artistic and cultural engagement. Some scientific research centers such as CERN have arts programs. In some cases, the arts and humanities are becoming a part of science education. This shift, where science is directly engaging the arts and humanities, reflects how more frequent collaborations are taking place across all fields of knowledge and practice.

Today's established art-science network is represented in arts installations, books and anthologies, popular magazines such as *Scientific American*, academic and literary journals, and more. Literary scholars have long addressed the art-science connection, sometimes through their teaching in addition to publications. For example, literary theorist N. Katherine Hayles, known for her scholarship on the relationship between literature, science, and technology, has co-taught combined literature-science classes at Duke University with Mark C. Kruse. I first met Mark as a visitor to one of their classes, talking about poems of mine that the class had read and speaking about quantum poetics. Academic organizations such as the Society for Literature, Science, and the Arts support scholarship and creative work across the arts and natural sciences.

In collaboration with others, I've established a global collective called The Entanglements Network, comprised of poets, scholars, artists, and scientists who are exploring innovative connections between poetry, science, and the arts. In the US, poet Ed Roberson, an *Entanglements* cofounder, draws from his early work experience in science-oriented fields alongside African American poetics and ecopoetics. Rae Armantrout, a recipient of the Pulitzer Prize for Poetry and an *Entanglements* cofounder, has over seventy poems about physics. *Entanglements* cofounder Will Alexander, as well as Mei-mei Berssenbrugge and former

US Poet Laureate Tracy K. Smith, are among other poets today who centrally position scientific knowledge in their poetry.

Though it's not common, other poets besides me work in scientific laboratories. Eduardo Kac and Christian Bök have worked with scientists to encode DNA proteins with language inside biological systems. Adam Dickinson practices what he calls metabolic poetics, writing poems about the pollutants he has in his own microbiome. S. S. Prasad combines poetry with science and technology by integrating nano-dimensions, dimensions beyond what can be seen with the naked eye, onto poetic text by using silicon microchips, which are usually used for computing. He was inspired by scientist Ghim Wei Ho. She works on silicon nanostructures through microscopic photos that she calls "nanoflowers." Prasad wrote a computer code inside her microchips that replaces the numbers with words, creating poems that are byproducts of the chip design.

Throughout literary history writers have engaged science, including major figures such as Margaret Cavendish, Johann Wolfgang von Goethe, Edgar Allan Poe, T. S. Eliot, and A. R. Ammons. Scientists such as Ernst Haeckel and Santiago Ramón y Cajal became artists as they conducted experiments in biology, artistically rendering what they saw. Today, artists, writers, and scientists continue to pursue connections between art and science.

Some scientists are also accomplished poets and writers. For example, astroparticle physicist Juan José Gómez Cadenas is a published novelist and poet who helped translate some of Rae Armantrout's poetry for a Spanish edition of one of her books. Ecologist and climate scientist Madhur Anand is a published poet who uses her own scientific articles in her poems. She was one of ten featured presenters whom I invited to *Entanglements: A Conference on the Intersections of Poetry, Science, and the Arts*, which I convened at Wake Forest.

Despite the headway that is being made at these interdisciplinary intersections, the most innovative work being done at the art-science nexus rarely captures the attention of the most visible and resourced communities in science, art, and literature. But the potential for this work to have larger impacts on society is strong.

In quantum poetics, *potentia* itself is a central principle, though it's not limited to Aristotle's idea of *potentia* as change and process. Theoreti-

10 | THE IMAGINARY PRESENT

cal physicist Werner Heisenberg, cofounder of quantum theory, says that "matter is in itself not a reality but only a possibility, a 'potentia'; it exists only by means of form." Through form, he says, matter "passes over" from possibility "into actuality."[3] Yet even form is not matter's essence, since nature, Heisenberg also suggests, can be defined only by the questions we ask of it.[4] Potency is another name that Aristotle gave *potentia*, and poetry as *potentia* may be the most *potent* question of all. Quantum poetics sees poetry as possibility in *potentia*, as imagination made material through form. In this way, poetry acts upon matter as both a figurative and a physical force, as both a symbolic and a material push or pull on matter that changes matter's motion. Poetry moves us.

Because of its special relationship to language and thinking, poetry is poised to respond to a question that science on its own has been unable to answer. That question is, What does quantum physics mean? Quantum poetics takes this question on by harnessing poetry as an artistic form of language that can both enact and interpret physics. In physics and poetry, time is not an arrow following a trajectory through a human past, present, and future. In physics and poetry, time is spacetime, combining the dimension of time with the three dimensions of space in one manifold known as the fourth dimension. In relativity, spacetime warps the spacetime in its vicinity, which, in turn, warps it. When poets are alert to how spacetime behaves, they can work with the spacetime on the page, or in any other medium, with greater critical and artistic intention. Similarly, when scientists are alert to how poets and artists experiment with spacetime, they can pursue science with broader perspectives. When we see science from a poet's viewpoint and poetry from a scientist's viewpoint, we can think like poets and scientists at the same time, drawing from their shared intelligence and imagination.

In his speculative essay "How to Construct a Time Machine" (1899), combining scientific and poetic thinking, Alfred Jarry proposes an "*Imaginary Present*" for which this book is named. The *Imaginary Present* in Jarry's essay is a second, symmetrical present that happens alongside the "real" present at the center between a future and a past that is traveled by an Explorer in a time machine. The Explorer in Jarry's time machine experiences two pasts, the "real" past and the *Imaginary Present*, which is the past created by the machine traveling from the future back to the "real" present. The Explorer in the time machine experiences time as a curve, a prescient idea by Jarry that the field of physics soon confirmed, when scientists discovered not only that space and time are one but that spacetime is curved.

Jarry's *Imaginary Present*, created by a time machine on its way back from the future to the "real" present, is an act of *poiesis*, the Ancient Greek word for "making" that led to the word poetry. By existing alongside the "real" present, the *Imaginary Present* subverts the assumed authority of the "real" present with an alternative spacetime made by technology, which is the time machine imagined in Jarry's book, as well as the essay itself. Duration, the time during which something continues, and which constitutes the experience of time by the Explorer, is a construct of memory at the continuous moment of its becoming in the *Imaginary Present*.[5] Since Jarry's *Imaginary Present* is a phenomenon of a second past occurring at the endless moment of a novel now, it contains the future as it's being constructed. Or, as poet Emily Dickinson has said, "Forever—is composed of—Nows." Jarry's *Imaginary Present* is created by a technology using rational and creative thinking together. Like quantum poetics, it travels.

Writing the Speed of Light

The more I apply principles of physics to poetry, the more I question the spacetime of my own poems. I also have new questions of the poems I'm reading: How is gravity behaving? How is language interacting with space and time? Broader questions surface: Poetry is a form of travel, but can we say that poetry travels space and time? What are the implications of using language for artistic purposes in a universe where the farther we look into space, the farther we are looking back into time?

By this I mean: Telescopes are time machines.

When we look into outer space from our relative position on Earth, we're looking back into time by viewing objects in space as they existed in the past. Since these objects are viewed by us when their light arrives to Earth, the version of these objects we have yet to see is in our future. Since it takes about eight minutes for the light from the Sun to reach our eyes, its originary light is slightly in our past. Likewise, when we are seen by an observer, we are not only being observed as we were slightly in our past, the version of ourselves that has yet to be observed, but which exists in our present, is in the observer's future. Light, like poetry, travels.

If we were to be seen on Earth by an observer in outer space, we would exist in that observer's past, just as objects in space exist in our past. Since each object in the universe exists in both the future and past of other objects, but never quite in an absolute present that we often assume exists equally for all things, the "real" present does not independently exist. This is because of the delay in light travel, which, according to Albert Einstein's theory of special relativity, occurs throughout the universe. Nothing travels faster than light, except, perhaps, the quantum states of entangled subatomic particles. But what about poetry? Poetry travels through readers, and readers travel through poetry. Does poetry travel faster than light?

Writing the Speed of Light | 13

Despite the delay in light travel that makes everything that we observe on Earth and in outer space a part of our past, we measure how far away objects are from one another with units such as miles and meters, but these units do not consider how far away from us objects are in time. We have separate measurements for time, using units such as minutes and seconds that are both practically and conceptually disconnected from units of space. When measuring objects in outer space, scientists understand that space and time must be treated together, since space-time, as discovered in relativity, is a unified manifold made of the three dimensions of space intersecting with the one dimension of time. In science, this manifold that combines space with time is known as the fourth dimension.

The determination of how far away an object is from Earth is made by scientists observing that object's redshift, which is measured by calculating the expansion of the universe in relation to the object's light spectrum. The unit of measurement that is used to describe the distance of objects from Earth, a unit of spacetime, is known as light-years, an often hyphenated word made by combining a unit of space (light) with a unit of time (years). In cosmology, a light-year is the distance that light travels in one Earth year in the vacuum of space.

Scientists know that subatomic particles make up all matter. Quantum theory asserts that when subatomic particles are measured by an apparatus or observer, the apparatus or observer affects their position and momentum. Consequently, the future position and momentum of particles can be predicted only in probabilities instead of certainties. This is the core concept within quantum theory's famous principle of indeterminacy, known as the uncertainty principle. In the discovery of how spacetime behaves at cosmological scales in relativity, and in the discovery of how particles of matter behave at subatomic scales in quantum theory, language plays a key but undervalued role. Since poetry works with language in uncommon ways, poetry invites new forms of thinking about physical phenomena. My work as a poet applies this artistic relationship that poets have with language to open questions in physics, the branch of the natural sciences that describes the structure of matter and how the fundamental parts of the universe interact. I do so by considering the often unacknowledged intersections of poetry and science when studying physics and visiting scientific research centers. I call this prac-

14 | THE IMAGINARY PRESENT

tice "quantum poetics," since I focus on quantum theory in my studies. I also engage quantum theory in my poetics, the theories and principles that inform reading, writing, and literary interpretation.

Quantum poetics asks: Under the ambiguities of spacetime and matter that physics such as relativity and quantum theory reveal, is it possible to describe what is happening? In her book-length poems *Happily* (2000) and *The Fatalist* (2003), poet-critic Lyn Hejinian writes, "This is happening" and "All that happened is what is happening."[1] Is it possible to describe what is happening? This is a question about what defines the parameters of language in relation to reality. It is also a question about how what is happening is not only what is happening from a human perspective but also what is happening outside of what we can observe. It is a question that addresses what appears to be happening through different orientations in space and time, including the spacetime of poetry.

According to the theory of the Big Bang, as well as empirical data from scientific evidence, the universe has been expanding from a dimensionless point of extreme density and temperature for 13.8 billion years. Matter, gravity, and electromagnetic forces coalesced in the early universe, introducing novel configurations of matter that would eventually form objects such as solar systems. New compositions in the universe, including new poems and artworks, represent an increase in both spatial and temporal complexity, one that takes place as the universe expands, which scientists have discovered it is doing at accelerating rates. Ethnobotanist Terence McKenna once proposed that the most novel form of matter in the universe is situated behind our eyes.[2] If his hypothesis is accurate, the phenomenon of cosmic novelty is a trait and force of evolution. When novelty is expressed through the action of language in the literary artform of poetry, which is an activity of thinking joined with perception, novelty becomes one way of understanding human consciousness and what we perceive to be happening.

In *Art & Physics: Parallel Visions in Space, Time, and Light* (2001), neurosurgeon Leonard Shlain explains how while Euclid articulated linear space, Aristotle articulated linear time. Euclid codified the concept of space into a field of knowledge, where abstract thought is conceived through diagrams. In Euclidean geometry, space is organized as if its points could be connected by an imaginary web of straight lines that do not actually exist in the natural world. Just as imaginary lines in nature became the key to Euclidean space, Shlain points out, concepts such as sequence, duration, past, present, and future became the key to Aristotelian time. Based on his notions of linear time and Euclid's notions of linear space, Aristotle developed rules of logic and problem-solving techniques using syllogisms, "if-then" hypotheses.[3]

Euclidean space and Aristotelian time have had a major influence on Western civilization, including on the development of classical mechanics, also known as Newtonian physics. Classical mechanics is based on the scientific method, which requires if-then hypotheses to be tested through experimentation, observation, and analysis. Shlain explains that like other mathematical formulations in physics such as quantum mechanics, which are the mathematical laws that govern subatomic particles in quantum theory, Isaac Newton's classical mechanics aims to systematically describe the universe in mathematical relationships.[4]

Shlain argues that in Western civilization, breakthroughs in physics have often happened near the same time as similar breakthroughs in the visual arts. For example, around the same time that Renaissance painters developed perspective through a single vanishing point—which gave the field of visual art the third dimension of depth, rejecting the flat depictions of space and time that were common for years in the medieval art of the Dark Ages—classical mechanics arose from measuring the natural world through observations, which were dependent on realistic perspectives. Similarly, Shlain continues, Einstein developed his theory of special relativity, which describes the relationship of space and time, within a few years of artists Pablo Picasso and Georges Braque developing cubism, the modernist visual art movement that experiments with space, time, and form.[5]

Shlain proposes that Einstein's relativity asked questions that usurped thousands of years of Euclidean space and Aristotelian time by offering a new framework by which to understand how space and time interact.[6] According to theoretical physicist Michio Kaku in *Physics of the Impossible* (2008), one of the most important questions that Einstein asked is, How would the world look to someone sitting astride a beam of light?[7]

16 | THE IMAGINARY PRESENT

while light travels
in a straight line
  at the speed of light
the poem written astride it
  would not
and while the world would no longer be
  the world
      (and it never was)
  at the speed of light
    the world would appear
  spare   infinitely   thin
      like a piece of paper
        viewed
          from an edge:
            "all
            here"
          all
        when
          where
          there are no pre-
          positions

Shlain illustrates how Picasso and Braque, through cubism, and Einstein, through relativity, imagined that all points in space along a path of observation simultaneously occupy the same location. In his theory of general relativity, Einstein explained how the world might look to someone with access to all perspectives at the same time, collapsing the ordinary distinctions between space and time.[8] We can see how in early cubist art such as Braque's *Pedestal Table* (1911), objects are viewed from multiple angles at the same time, fractured into visual fragments and rearranged so that the viewer does not have to move through space, in time, to view multiple angles of the objects in a linear sequence. While the viewer sees different angles or sides of the object at the same time on the canvas, they remain stationary, reversing a more typical experience with sculpture in fourth-dimensional spacetime, where a viewer must move around an object in time to see all or most of its angles or sides.[9]

In relativity, for the person sitting astride a beam of light, the frames of reference ahead, behind, and to the side, directions pointed to grammatically in English by prepositions (evoked by "pre-/positions" in my poem above), merge, suggesting a different kind of spacetime that is, in Shlain's description, and in my poem, "infinitely thin" and "all here."[10] The phrase "all here" is also "all when" and "all where," a poetic spacetime collapsing into an imperceptible point of zero dimension, or what can be conceptualized as all dimensions, for a viewer sitting astride a beam of light. This point of zero dimension would contain everything in its nothingness.

In both relativity and cubism, space and time are relative and inseparable, uniting in what was then a newly discovered dimension, the fourth dimension. This discovery accompanied a new word, a portmanteau, that combined space and time into *spacetime*, which, like light-years, is sometimes hyphenated, sometimes not. In the radical thinking that emerged from relativity in the field of physics and cubism in the field of visual art in the early twentieth century, Euclidean and Aristotelian ideas about space and time became outdated, no longer applying to all scales of physical reality, yet commonly held ideas about reality often assume these ideas are truths.

What Shlain did not acknowledge is that poets make similar discoveries as scientists and visual artists. Poets do so by drawing upon the creative possibilities of language. Poets create not only new configurations of words, images, and sounds but new units of measurement—poems— for how artistic language interacts with the physics of spacetime.

The Multiverse

While Leonard Shlain convincingly argues for the connections between cubism and relativity in *Art & Physics*, he doesn't address how they relate to literature. For example, just as spatial repetitions in cubist art collapse sequential notions of space and time by evoking simultaneity—similar to how in relativity space and time are one manifold—temporal repetitions in the textual space of Gertrude Stein's writing evoke the simultaneity of space and time.

In Stein's literary portrait of Pablo Picasso in her prose poem "Three Portraits of Painters" (1912), space expands through the repetition of words and phrases that move through reiterations of time, achieved as the poem builds. One result of this textual interaction between space and time is the emergence of a new spacetime on the page, a fitting result for the poem, which presents Picasso bringing a mysterious "thing" out of himself. Stein describes this thing that Picasso brings out of himself as "a heavy thing, a solid thing and a complete thing," pointing to poiesis, the act of making things.[1] The root of the English noun poetry is the Ancient Greek term *poi*, which means "to make," a verb that led to poiesis. As a poet, I know that poetry is both a noun and the underground verb at its root. The word root comes from the Latin *radicalis*, which led to the word radical, the condition of fundamental change and reform. The most innovative writers, like the most innovative scientists, challenge existing ideas toward radical change and reform.

The alternative spacetime of poiesis, like many works of cubism and experimental writing, operates where the first, second, and third dimensions of space are joined with the dimension of time in the fourth dimension, represented by temporal repetition in Stein's writing and spatial repetition in cubist art. Literary works like Stein's, which function under the poetic logic of quantum physics as opposed to the Newtonian logic of

18 |

classical mechanics, illustrate novel ways to treat so-called paradoxes and contradictions by refusing to resolve them.

Spacetime, as conceived of in relativity, and its expressions in literary artworks like Stein's writing, interacts with other phenomena such as gravity. According to Shlain's description of relativity, light binds space, time, matter, and energy, and the interplay between these forces results in gravity. In relativity, space is not empty, and matter does not inertly move through space. Matter tells spacetime how to warp the spacetime in its vicinity. Likewise, warped spacetime tells matter how to behave.[2] This can explain why the interaction between space, time, and matter in Stein's writing, bound by light that travels to Earth from the Sun, results in a density of artistic force, a high level of gravity, which compresses matter.

In quantum theory, which emerges ten to fifteen years after general relativity, other radical revisions to common understandings of space and time occur. In addition to the observer affecting what is being observed in quantum theory, subatomic matter is thought to swerve in and out of observation, moving by what's known as the quantum jump outside of the law of deterministic causality, commonly known as cause and effect. In quantum theory, the building blocks of all matter, subatomic particles, are in simultaneous states of space and time in what's known as quantum superposition before coming into existence as defined states.

While relativity and quantum theory challenge classical mechanics, there is a problem with relativity and quantum theory being compatible models of physical reality. Relativity breaks down at quantum scales of space and time. Quantum theory breaks down at relativistic scales of space and time. In quantum theory, the relationship of the observed and the observer is made new, but classical conceptions of space and time are retained. In relativity, space and time are made new, but classical conceptions of the observed and the observer are retained.[3] Physicists are attempting to develop a single theory of physical reality, a quantum field theory, that allows for both relativity and quantum physics. This theory will likely contain a theory for quantum gravity. Theories of quantum gravity are known as unified field theories, based on field-theory physics, and some are referred to as M-theory, short for membrane theory.

One of the best-known unified field theories of quantum gravity is superstring theory. In superstring theory, spacetime is an ambiguous ecology where our universe is part of a larger wilderness, a multiverse

20 | THE IMAGINARY PRESENT

that is comprised of multiple, and perhaps infinite, dimensions of space-time. Quantum poetics treats poetry as a multiversal literary art, invoking invisible ecosystems at subatomic and astronomical scales, ambiguous spacetimes, and collisions between membranes or borders. In superstring theory, the multiple dimensions of spacetime that go beyond the fourth dimension are created by collisions between subatomic, vibrating membranes of energy, referred to as open and closed strings. Superstring theory is a good example of how scientists have to think as imaginatively as poets. Following in the tradition of Western atomic science from Thales to Democritus, superstring theorists hypothesize that strings are elementary particles, fundamental forms of matter that are thought to have no additional substructures.

Years ago, at the University of Colorado Boulder, I heard theoretical physicist Lisa Randall give a talk soon after she had visited CERN, just before the Large Hadron Collider (LHC) went operational. The LHC searches for new forms of matter by colliding subatomic particles, protons, underground at high speeds. She said that physicists think that gravity, unlike other forces in the universe such as electromagnetism, is present in all dimensions of a higher-dimensional model of the universe.[4] Asking us audience members to use our imaginations, she showed us rudimentary drawings of the open and closed strings in superstring theory. She showed us these drawings to illustrate the hypothesis that our universe may be a low-gravity universe, while other dimensions may be high-gravity universes. While Randall's talk was informative and inspiring, this moment in her presentation was a lost opportunity, and it points to a larger problem in how science is too often studied and communicated to broader audiences without directly engaging other fields such as literature and art.

When audiences who are not scientists are asked by scientists to use their imaginations to understand concepts in physics, physics gets closer to creative pursuits such as poetry and art. But the descriptions that scientists use could be as imaginative as the science itself. Even without formal training in literature and art, physicists must be imaginative in moving from mathematics into natural language through metaphor, analogy, and visual representation. This is partly because language and image, in the context of science, are often translations of mathematics, since language and image function as key conduits through which scientists think and communicate.

Description, however, is only one facet of language and image. Poets and artists know that language and image possess both descriptive and aesthetic power and that these properties are interrelated. If Randall had shown a poem or visual artwork that evoked the subatomic, vibrating membranes of energy that define the open and closed strings in superstring theory, which she wanted us in her audience to imaginatively visualize, we would not only better understand these ideas, we would materially encounter poetry or image as subatomic strings, experiencing them not only as concept but matter. Art and poetry can evoke the topological characteristics of open strings (lines), closed strings (circles), and energy (vibration). Art and poetry also can present units of image and language resembling the different forms of gravity that Randall wanted to depict that day—high and low—as she was making distinctions between our universe and other dimensions theorized by physicists. Paintings by Marc Chagall, for example, where objects often appear to float within settings aligned with non-Euclidean space, unhinged from an Earth-like gravity, evoke a low-gravity universe. Gertrude Stein's "Three Portraits of Painters" evokes a high-gravity universe with its density of spacetime created through linguistic repetition. Did Chagall and Stein deliberately craft their artworks with the low- and high-gravity universes of superstring theory in mind? No, because superstring theory hadn't yet been formulated. However, by using poetic thinking, each produced artworks that express gravitational force in ways that speak to the high and low gravity of different universes in superstring theory. Chagall and Stein made their artworks using poetic vision, demonstrating how new ways of seeing reality are made possible through the imagination.

The value of integrating literary and visual art with science has benefits beyond education. Art is the material matter of imagination and can help bring critical and creative depth to science. Similarly, artists and writers benefit in engaging science by bringing more critical and creative depth to their poetic vision. Collaborations between the arts and sciences can occur across practice and theory. Quantum poetics is itself one type of collaboration.

The New Spacetime

The uncertainty principle in quantum theory changed the way that knowledge is defined. One way it achieved this is by demonstrating that the behavior of matter, and its momentum and position in spacetime, can be predicted only through probability instead of certainty. In *Physics and Philosophy* (1958), Werner Heisenberg says that after quantum theory, it is no longer accurate, when considering the behavior of the subatomic particles that the theory describes, to speak in terms of what is "known" or "not known." Instead, he says, we need to speak in terms of what is "decided" or "not decided."[1] Deciding on the properties of a subatomic particle is far different than knowing them, for a decision is involved instead of the uncovering of truth. Knowing the properties of a subatomic particle, or knowing anything, assumes that certainty or absolute knowledge can be achieved, since one way of seeing knowledge is that it is understanding verified by fact or empirical evidence. But deciding on the properties of subatomic particles in quantum theory suggests that any description of any subject of study rests not on knowledge or certainty but on interpretation, which requires imagination.

What Heisenberg understood, and what my work in quantum poetics seeks to expand, is that quantum theory reveals the limitations of classical physics and its Newtonian language to accurately describe the universe and what is happening. Newtonian language, based on the inheritances of classical mechanics and the scientific method, which drew from Aristotelian time and Euclidean space, is the language of prose without attention to the artistry of form. After the development of quantum theory, the language that is used to describe it, Heisenberg suggests, must markedly change.[2] Similarly, quantum poetics suggests that what constitutes knowledge when using language must also be made new to account for quantum theory's discoveries.

Quantum theory has already produced important complications to the concept of language. In cases when poetic form, which we can imagine as the poem's body, and poetic content, which we can imagine as the poem's mind, are an interactive whole, the environment with which a poem is written, such as a page, is indistinguishable from the poem itself. In other words, the environment in which a poem is written is an intrinsic part of the poem's material existence. To interpret a poem, therefore, is to see it in relation to its setting. This setting is conceptual but also physical. Interpretation involves decision making, requiring creative thinking, as opposed to certainty or absolute knowledge. Quantum theory, therefore, is a theory within science that partly functions like the arts and humanities.

Many of the physicists whom I have met say that while they understand how to apply quantum theory, they cannot say what it means. Yet, because of their intellectual and creative capacities, physicists are in a strong position to consider quantum theory, both as scientists through critical thinking and as artists through poetic vision. Unlike those working in the arts and humanities who are trained in using interpretation to arrive at meaning, scientists are usually not trained to interpret the meaning of science. As a result of these educational limitations, science has failed to contend with the conceptual complexities that quantum theory presents. When I began studying quantum theory as a poet, it was my training and experience that allowed me to recognize its apparent contradictions and paradoxes as forms of poetic logic. Given how ambiguity and abstraction in poetry serve its artistry, a phenomenon such as quantum superposition appears to operate with poetic logic. Poetry is subject to the same so-called counter-logic that guides the behavior of the subatomic particles that constitute it.

When there are references to poetry in science, more often than not, they are metaphors, similes, or analogies used to demonstrate a scientific concept or bring value to it. When there are references to science in poetry, the poem often uses science as a symbol or representation of an idea. But literary devices using methods of comparision can go only so far. Writers and artists, for example, are often unaware of the double-slit experiment, since they are usually not educated in physics. If they were educated in physics, they could consider the philosophical dimensions of the experiment, which demonstrates how a photon, a quantum particle of light, can be both a particle of matter and a wave of energy, depending

24 | THE IMAGINARY PRESENT

on how it is measured or observed. Similarly, writers and artists rarely consider the phenomenon of quantum entanglement, where the quantum states of subatomic particles, separated after once being near, "communicate," influencing each other by exchanging information faster than the speed of light. If more writers and artists were educated in how phenomena such as quantum entanglement and wave-particle duality work, they could apply this understanding to the making of their art.

Just like the belief in absolute knowledge that is still promoted in the more conventional corners of science, the conventional corners of the arts and humanities can be essentialist, proceeding as if universal truth exists. Totalizing gestures in science, like those in the arts and humanities, usually lack intellectual and imaginative rigor. In art that is influenced by postmodernism, for example, totalizing gestures are challenged by emphasizing the speculative over the absolute, the partial over the whole, the fleeting over the fixed, and the constructed over the authentic. Conventional science, or any domain of culture that promotes absolute knowledge, can be better challenged by responding to the poetic dimensions of physics such as quantum theory.

A new paradigm may be possible where poetry and physics coexist in dialogue and experimentation, not toward unification but toward an active exchange of ideas and debate within the expanded spectrum of their constituent parts. This interdisciplinary paradigm would have a positive impact on society by challenging entrenched systems of thinking in science, art, religion, education, and politics. Such a paradigm could also help disrupt our addiction to searching for exact laws and conclusive meaning, a pathology often steeped in a narrowness of mind that can lead to bigotry, exploitation, and violence.

When certainty is acknowledged as a ruin of ignorance, the pursuit of knowledge will happen with a better understanding that all discoveries are provisional. In the new spacetime of quantum poetics, space and time, like form and content in a poem, are co-creative. Poetic thinking overcomes the illusion of fixed binaries by being quantum, and not superficially in metaphor, analogy, or symbolism but as an invariant state of the possible.

'Pataphysics Is an Iridescent Veil

An early influence on my work in quantum poetics is Alfred Jarry, founder of 'pataphysics, a "science of imaginary solutions" where exceptions are the rule.[1] Jarry conceived of 'pataphysics to challenge the artistic, scientific, political, and cultural standards of his time. The inaugural performance of his play *Ubu Roi* (1896), loosely based on Shakespeare's *Macbeth* (1606), was a scathing critique of power and the bourgeoisie. Its performance was incendiary to his late nineteenth-century audience. Fanciful stage settings and a poetic preamble by Jarry startled the audience just before the actor playing the main character shouted the play's first word, merdre, an appropriated version of merde, or "shit." While merdre was also used to mean "good luck," a public utterance of the word would have been unacceptable. Pandemonium in the theater ensued after the word was spoken, and many abruptly walked out, openly offended.[2]

Poet Guillaume Apollinaire was in the audience that night and later proclaimed Jarry's play a masterpiece. He was one of the first writers to defend the experimental nature of cubism from criticism when he spoke about the "new possibilities of spatial measurement, which in the language of the modern studios are designated by the term, fourth dimension."[3] Jarry's poetic vision influenced Apollinaire, poet André Breton, and others in their development of Surrealism, the literary and artistic movement that explores the subconscious and dream worlds with the purpose of liberating the mind and, in turn, society through creative thinking.

One foundational concept in Jarry's pantheon of literary symbols is clinamen, a term first coined by Greek philosopher Epicurus and later reinterpreted by Roman philosopher Lucretius in his book-length poem *On the Nature of Things* (c. 99–55 BC). Lucretius refers to clinamen as the spontaneous swerving of atoms in space as they fall in a vertical path.[4]

| 25

26 | THE IMAGINARY PRESENT

The swerve of atoms from their trajectories, eternally in motion, was responsible for the creation of matter, Lucretius reasoned, since without this swerve, atoms would never touch and form matter. Later, clinamen was used to describe unpredictable departures from expectation. Literary scholar Roger Shattuck, one of Jarry's translators, notes that clinamen is expressed in the uncertainty principle in quantum theory.[5] In *The Anxiety of Influence* (1973), literary scholar Harold Bloom uses the term to talk about how writers swerve away from their predecessors.[6] Poet-critic Joan Retallack, in *The Poethical Wager* (2003), discusses the swerve of clinamen as a possible poetics.[7] More recent books use the concept of clinamen to track literary shifts in history.

In Jarry's novel *Exploits and Opinions of Doctor Faustroll, Pataphysician* (1911), clinamen is given physical form when painter Henri Rousseau, a character in the novel based on the artist, is in charge of an animated machine named Clinamen. The machine is described as a mechanical "beast" and "spinning top." Rousseau is to use it to alter the canvases hanging in a museum.[8] Clinamen awakens after an apocalypse, living in a world that it alone will create, endowed with divine power. It is described as ejaculating "on to the walls of its universe," the museum, with "primary colors ranged according to the tubes of its stomach."[9] It creates thirteen paintings, each depicted in the novel as a prose poem such as this one, titled "Love":

> The soul is wheeled by Love who looks exactly like an iridescent veil and assumes the masked face of a chrysalis. It walks upon inverted skulls. Behind the wall where it hides, claws brandish weapons. It is baptized with poison. Ancient monsters, the wall's substance, laugh into their green beards. The heart remains red and blue, violet in the artificial absence of the iridescent veil that it is weaving.[10]

Love is described as a veil created from luminous colors that change in different angles. It is a figure masked by the protective state of a transforming insect and linked with violence and death. The wall it hides behind is a border of ancient monsters who laugh into their beards, colored green by hallucinatory indulgences in what is a reference to wormwood-infused absinthe, a hallucinogen known as the Green Fairy, that Jarry drank. The heart of the soul that encounters this figure of love becomes as psychedelic as the iridescent veil that it weaves to coax the soul. The poem enacts Jarry's conception of clinamen by swerving into kaleidoscopic portrayals of love, death, and artifice. For Jarry, the imagination is an activity of clinamen. The more distanced the imagination is from standard thinking, the more it can swerve and disrupt.

The transformation of paintings into prose poems and the sudden interruption of prose poems in Jarry's novel serve as enactments of clinamen's unforeseen swerve and deviation from narrative protocol. Similarly, the content of the prose poems in the novel swerves from the primary narrative that chronicles the main character, Doctor Faustroll, and his adventures by introducing new situations that are dropped, never visited again.

Clinamen, as a concept, is envisioned by Jarry as a technology of the artist that subverts authority through hyperbole, surprise, chance, irreverence, and humor. As a painting machine and mechanical monster, Clinamen remakes the museum, which, for Jarry, symbolizes the authoritative, institutional setting of art that his writing and lifestyle worked to satirize and sabotage. That this machine is initially given to Rousseau, who, according to Shattuck, had a reputation for being so naïve that he was often the victim of cruel jokes, reinforces the notion that, for Jarry, clinamen is not another form of authority.[11] This is a key point in Jarry's interpretation of clinamen as a law of 'pataphysics. In her essay "A ≠ A: The Potential for a 'Pataphysical Poetic in Dan Farrell's *The Inkblot Record*" (2011), poet-critic Katie L. Price, speaking about 'pataphysical texts, explains that "rather than offering yet another alternative ideological frame, they allow us to think about the logic of framing."[12] 'Pataphysics challenges the ideological assumptions within the framing of scientific, literary, and philosophical thought.

Quantum poetics proposes that artforms such as poetry are material manifestations of clinamen, inviting an imaginative swerve to interrupt a path. As in relativity and quantum theory, clinamen's swerve usurps Aristotle's conceptions of time and Euclid's conceptions of space. In the creative swerve-logic of quantum poetics, developments in theoretical physics such as quantum theory show that swerves do not just happen at cultural or artistic levels but also within material reality. Not unlike the relationship between matter and spacetime in relativity, the spacetime of poetry acts upon spatiotemporal swerves, clinamens in space and

28 | THE IMAGINARY PRESENT

time. Just as swerves in space locate and dissipate words on the page in a poem, swerves in time can inspire and dissolve rhythm, adding artistic and material dimension to poetic language.

Like the relationship of the observed and the observer in quantum theory, where the observer affects what is being observed, a reader influences a text and a viewer influences an artwork. In both quantum theory and artforms such as poetry, meaning is a process rather than an end point. Swerves in spacetime within the material world of nature are creative actions that detach Aristotle's linear time from the imaginary web of straight lines in Euclid's geometry. This allows for new forms of conceptual and material spacetime to arise.

Gertrude Stein, in *Composition as Explanation* (1926), addresses the simultaneity of spacetime in a theory of narration, a poetic explanation of her composition and process as a writer, which she calls the "continuous present." She says, "Continuous present is one thing and beginning again and again is another thing. These are both things. And then there is using everything."[13] Similar to quantum superposition, where subatomic particles are simultaneously in every possible spacetime, Stein's continuous present is an every-thing occurring at the every-moment of the now-here. It begins again and again in the constant, creative reinvention of the present. Stein's continuous present is similar to Jarry's *Imaginary Present* in his essay "How to Construct a Time Machine," where a second, alternative present challenges the authority of the "real" present. This alternative present, the *Imaginary Present*, is made by a time machine as it travels from the future back to the "real" present, thus containing the future.[14]

In quantum theory, subatomic particles such as quarks and gluons in superposition, before coming into existence at the moment of observation or measurement, are thought to be elementary particles, just as atoms were once believed to be the most indivisible form of matter. In matrix mechanics, Werner Heisenberg's abstract mathematics that uses visual matrices to calculate quantum mechanical phenomena, the quantum properties of subatomic systems are governed by the uncertainty principle. The position and momentum of subatomic particles, in the uncertainty principle, can be described only in probabilities, not with certainty, because their present states cannot be known without ambiguity. In quantum theory, simultaneous values cannot be assigned to the position and momentum of subatomic particles in superposition. The particles move by quantum jump, an atomic swerve, not from cause and effect.

According to *Faust in Copenhagen* (2007) by physicist Gino Segrè, Heisenberg's mathematics, known as matrix mechanics, was original for developing what physicist Max Born called symbolic multiplication.[15] Born illustrated that the commutative law of arithmetic is not valid in subatomic systems. Commutation in mathematics is when one value equals another value regardless of where the value is placed in the equation. For example, $AB = BA$, or $4 \times 3 = 3 \times 4$.[16] But in subatomic systems, Born demonstrated, position times momentum does not equal momentum times position. This was a major departure from the thinking then. In Newtonian classical mechanics, all variables such as the position and momentum of an object commute.

Heisenberg also developed the work of physicist Max Planck, who established a relationship between mass and frequency. This led to what's known as Planck's constant, which defines how much energy can exist in the smallest and most elementary forms of matter. Since in quantum physics Planck's constant is always nonzero—it has to have a value of one or more—and since the position and momentum of subatomic particles is proportional to Planck's constant, uncertainty is always at play in observing subatomic phenomena.[17]

Heisenberg, in his formulation of quantum theory, represented the position and momentum of particles in a matrix, a grid-like form, because he thought that the frequencies of spectral lines emitted by atoms represented infinite matrices.[18] Like a poem, whose literary form can be modeled after its thematic content, Heisenberg modeled the form of his mathematics on the mechanical behavior of subatomic particles.

Quantum poetics suggests that poetry is a matrix mechanics of language. Poetry is an artistic branch of language but also its mathematical machinery. If the multiverse exists as a part of physical reality, we can think of poetry as a multiversal technology, a material mechanics within the multiverse that helps describe it. Like other technologies, poetry is a mechanical prosthetic of the imagination, merging materiality with creative cognition.

In physics, scientists cannot see a full picture of a subatomic particle at any given time. They use what is called projection to see what mat-

30 | THE IMAGINARY PRESENT

ter does at some scales of reality so that they can infer how it behaves at other scales of reality. The work of physics, therefore, uses partial states of knowledge. In dark energy research, for example, astrophysicists must use imagination to help fill in what they cannot directly observe. Like experimental poetry and visual art, a fractured picture of a subatomic particle in four-dimensions occurs because it is being observed in the four dimensions that we are biologically capable of experiencing as observers; the particle cannot be directly observed in quantum superposition, where it is in all possible forms at the same time. In quantum physics, a unified view of material reality is not possible with our biological systems and technology, much like interpretations of art can never lead to absolute understanding. In both quantum physics and artforms like poetry, realism is an illusion, a misunderstanding that the whole is being viewed when only the partial can be received. Realism, in its assumption that what is perceived is what is there, precludes what is possible.

The description of reality within discrete parts, or partial understanding, in quantum physics differs from the continuous change, or assumed realism, of Newtonian classical mechanics. The partial descriptions of reality in experimental art like cubism or poetry have more in common with quantum physics than the realism inherent in classical physics. Yet, as advanced as art may be in suggesting new ways to perceive and interpret reality, it often does not go far enough in rejecting received ideas about what space and time are and how they interact. Quantum poetics suggests that common understandings of space and time must be rejected if, according to Heisenberg, "what we observe is not nature in itself but nature exposed to our method of questioning."[19] When our method of questioning determines our observations, and when, as observers, we are part of what is being observed, our method of questioning needs both a physics and a poetics to account for the forms that scientific and literary questions take.

Third Mind

The inventor of the telescope, Galileo Galilei, was one of Albert Einstein's heroes because of the courage that Galileo had to go against religious doctrine by advocating for the Copernican system of the universe that decentered the Earth. Poet John Milton visited Galileo when Galileo was under house arrest for his scientific work, and Milton based his defense of free speech, the first of its kind, on Galileo's situation.[1] Even in the seventeenth century, poets and scientists were sometimes in communication, developing their ideas within interdisciplinary fellowship.

Einstein's foreword to an edition of Galileo's *Dialogue Concerning the Two Chief World Systems* (1632) provides insight as to why he was so opposed to quantum theory. One concept in quantum theory that Einstein challenged was the quantum jump, how subatomic particles move without cause and effect when they are in quantum superposition. Despite the extraordinary breakthroughs that Einstein made in seeing that space and time were not separate, he remained a champion of Newtonian classical logic when it came to the more unconventional aspects of quantum theory such as the quantum jump. In fact, Einstein viewed quantum theory as a throwback to the days before the Age of Enlightenment in Western civilization, when rationality was suppressed by religious systems, such as during Galileo's lifetime.

While Einstein's defense of rationality in the context of received authority is admirable, it got in the way of his making the necessary imaginative leaps to accept the poetic logic inherent within quantum theory. In contrast, his contemporaries Niels Bohr and Werner Heisenberg championed the unconventional logic required of quantum theory. They also examined the implications of quantum theory in relationship to language. Heisenberg, in particular, understood that quantum theory is subject to its own principles, and any claims within its scope must be

31

THE IMAGINARY PRESENT

critically subject to uncertainty. In *Physics and Philosophy*, he discusses the problem with the law of *tertium non datur*, where it is assumed that there is no third option in a choice between two binaries. Heisenberg says that the law of *tertium non datur* must be modified in quantum theory, that there is always a third choice between the statements "Here is a table" and "Here is not a table."[2] In the Copenhagen interpretation of quantum theory, the law of *tertium non datur* is rejected. The subatomic particles in a table exist in a quantum superposition of all states in spacetime until the quantum state of each particle's wave function—the mathematical description of a particle's quantum state—collapses when observed or measured. This is the moment when the table's subatomic particles come into a defined state of existence.

In the Many-Worlds Interpretation of quantum theory, first proposed by physicist Hugh Everett, a particle never comes out of quantum superposition, since the wave function of a particle is thought to never collapse. Instead, every observation of the particle creates a new universe. While such a theory may seem outlandish within common conceptions of reality, it is a legitimate yet controversial theory in physics today and has many supporters among top scientists, including some I have met. In quantum theory, whether the wave function of a subatomic system collapses or not upon observation or measurement cannot be ultimately "known" with certainty, or, in Heisenberg's important term, "decided."[3]

Today, quantum theory remains at odds with relativity. In Heisenberg's lectures in Chicago, collected in *The Physical Principles of the Quantum Theory*, first published in 1930, he points out that Einstein's relativity "still divides the world into subject and object (observer and observed) and hence a clear formation of the law of causality."[4] The law of *tertium non datur*, that there can never be a third option between binaries, supports the dominant Cartesian subject-object dichotomy, separating the subject from the object that the subject acts upon. Crucially, Heisenberg's rejection of the law of *tertium non datur* emphasized that language, which is how mathematics is often conceptualized, is essential to understanding the meaning of quantum physics.[5] Heisenberg explored the problem of meaning when paradigms change. Outdated ideas need to fall away, he argued, to allow for "the resolution of the paradoxes of atomic physics [that] can be accomplished only by further renunciation of old and cherished ideas. Most important of these is the idea that natural phenomenon obey exact laws—the principle of causality. In fact, our ordinary description of nature, and the idea of exact laws, rests on the assumption that it is possible to observe the phenomena without appreciably influencing them."[6]

One way to allow for the so-called contradictions in quantum physics is to redefine the axioms upon which the concept of contradiction rests. Using poetic logic, quantum poetics suggests that the rejection of the law of causality in quantum physics is rational. Einstein did not seem to possess the metacritical depth of Heisenberg and, as a result, didn't pursue the philosophical dimensions of quantum theory that are necessary to grasping its claims.

Einstein is hardly alone among physicists in not examining quantum theory in relation to language, philosophy, and art. Physicists who are not engaged with such domains, much like poets who are not engaged with science, narrow the kinds of questions that they are capable of formulating, the methods they use to explore such questions, and the assumptions they forge in the context of conducting their work. Like a quantum computer that computes with qubits, which can be one, a zero, or any quantum superposition of one and zero, as opposed to the binary bits of a digital computer that computes using only with ones and zeros, a third option, a third field across poetry and science is also possible. Quantum poetics is one such possible third field. Like a third eye, or like writer William S. Burroughs and artist Brion Gysin's artistic collaborations that they called a "third mind," it negates the binary law of *tertium non datur* by being quantum. This rationally allows one thing to be two things at once in a third thing. The third thing—like Pablo Picasso's thing that Gertrude Stein says he brings out of himself and which she describes as "a heavy thing, a solid thing and a complete thing" in "Three Portraits of Painters"—is both the two things and the third thing created by the quantum dialectic of the binary.

The Imaginary Present

Much of Alfred Jarry's fiction can be situated within the setting of the *Imaginary Present*, a theory of spacetime that he proposes in his essay "How to Construct a Time Machine." The *Imaginary Present* is a second present to the "real" present that is made by a time machine as it travels from the future back to the "real" present.

One example of how Jarry uses the *Imaginary Present* is in his last novel *The Supermale* (1902). The male protagonist, André Marcueil, tests the limits of human will by having sex with a consenting woman, Ellen Elson, eighty-two times before turning into a machine, called the Supermale. While Ellen loves André, André does not love Ellen; he merely "adores" her. Ellen's father, upset by André's lack of love for his daughter, has him hooked up to an electromagnetic machine designed to mechanically produce his love. Attached to the machine and looked after by a doctor named Bathybius, André transforms into the Supermale but still only "adores" Ellen instead of loving her. In a typical Jarry inversion that wildly moves past the limits of plausibility, the machine is then described as falling in love with André, who, as the Supermale, escapes it. After getting twisted in the ironwork at the house's gate as he attempts to leave, he dies.

The final sentence of the novel describes how Ellen found a jeweler to set one of the Supermale's solid, mechanical tears into a ring, in the place of a pearl, to symbolize the "real" love that they never had.[1] That the mechanical tear, unlike a "real" pearl, is the absence of love suggests that Jarry is highlighting the difference between the authentic pearl of love and the mechanical tear of adoration, which becomes Ellen's pathological substitute for unrequited love.

Bathybius, a figure who represents scientific authority in the novel, says that "man" created "God," not the other way around. "He [God] is

34

The Imaginary Present | 35

greater than all dimensions, without being beyond dimension; neither immaterial or infinite. He is only indefinite."[2] Jarry is distinguishing the indefinite, that which cannot be defined or is undefined, from the immaterial, that which does not have physical existence. He also is distinguishing the indefinite from the infinite, time without end. The divine science of Bathybius resembles how, in the Copenhagen interpretation of quantum theory, a subatomic particle in quantum superposition exists in an indefinite rather than an immaterial, or infinite, spacetime before being observed or measured when its quantum state collapses.

Later in *The Supermale*, the narrator says that "God is infinitely small," "a point," and "beyond all dimensions, but within," further relating the concept and location of the divine inside the physical structures of subatomic space.[3] The cells of human sperm and ova are described as goddesses and gods who unite and "bring with them, each from his [their] own side, the one toward the other, the world they inhabit," creating a new world. This "passive inevitability" is called "love," a result of the sperm and ovum making a new world.[4] That Ellen and André never produce offspring from their sexual encounters is symbolic of André's lack of love for Ellen, but the procreation that never happens also points to the idea that love produces not only new beings but new worlds, which are ecologies, like the novel itself, arising from a creative act.

Despite *The Supermale* being set in Jarry's future, the time and place of the novel, its ecological world, are disconnected from ordinary settings of time and space, a common feature in Jarry's worldview within the *Imaginary Present*. That spacetime is so fluid in Jarry's work speaks to his instructions on how to build a time machine in his essay, where the present moment of "reality" is accompanied by another present, one that is imaginary and thus indefinitely more "real" in its poetic construction, and where neither operates beyond perception outside of the act of making in poeisis. Further, Jarry's second present to the "real" present, the *Imaginary Present*, evokes how quantum theory treats the observer as part of the ecology of what is being observed. These reorientations define space and time as constructs linked to perception. Perception itself is intertwined with any measurement that depends on observation for meaning.

Most everything in Jarry's literary world foregrounded the constructed qualities of time, space, and reality. Jarry's *Imaginary Present* that

36 | THE IMAGINARY PRESENT

runs alongside the present of the "real" is a literary precursor to the extra dimensions posited in superstring theory. He used the term 'pataphysics to mediate the flux of reality between the "real" present and the *Imaginary Present*. 'Pataphysics is a science of imaginary solutions, he says, that examines the laws "governing exceptions."[5] It "will explain the universe supplementary to this one" and "will describe a universe which can be— and perhaps should be—envisaged in the place of the traditional one."[6] Claiming that 'pataphysics is the physics that explains the laws of this other universe, Jarry presciently addresses scientific theories to come, such as multiple universes.

In Jarry's philosophical system, the traditional universe is replaced by a universe that uses 'pataphysics rather than physics or metaphysics as its guiding science, and as a result, Jarry's science has poetic properties. Much like Werner Heisenberg's critique of "exact laws,"[7] Jarry's 'pataphysical multiverse works outside of what is absolute. Jarry presents the extreme conditions of the Supermale's desires to explore the aspects of humankind where exceptions are the rule, where imaginary solutions are what's "real," and where the impossible becomes possible, all properties of the world that are at play in quantum theory and poetry. For Jarry, what prevents these ideal conditions of creativity from flourishing is the rigidity, authority, and arrogance of human culture and its conventional science, literature, politics, and art.

In *The Supermale*, André, before he is hooked up to the machine that is supposed to make him love Ellen, suggests to Bathybius that if a man is capable of "making love indefinitely," then a man could do any number of things indefinitely.[8] Bathybius rebuts this suggestion by saying, "Science has other convictions on that matter. . . . Anywhere other than in the department of the impossible, which scientists do not admit, as they have no chair in it, energies can only develop if they are specialized— and even then not indefinitely!"[9] In 'pataphysics, the "department of the impossible" is a new anti-administrative structure to contend with science's imaginative subject matter. There is no chairperson, no leader, no structural authority in the department of the impossible, which operates outside of the orthodoxies of power and culture.

If social reality is both a linguistic and physical construct, if space and time are one manifold, and if Heisenberg is accurate in saying that it's "a matter of personal belief whether . . . a calculation concerning the past history of [an] electron can be ascribed any physical reality or not,"[10] then the time machine in Jarry's essay already exists. The essay "How to Construct a Time Machine" contains a (space)time machine, but it itself is also a machine of (space)time.

The Supermale's
solid tear is worn

in her ring like a
perpetual heart

of both the machine
and the woman

who fell in love
with the man

'shadow, neither
immaterially nor

infinitely but
indefinitely, a god-

dess embracing
past light records

in proximity to
the other starlike

world they create—
the department

of the impossible—
I, too, adore

The Reader as a Quantum Observer

In literary theory, reader-response criticism says that a reader's interpretation of a text should be given equal or greater authority over the author's intention. Similar claims have been made by theorists and practitioners associated with L=A=N=G=U=A=G=E poetry, a literary movement that emphasizes the necessity of open interactions with creative texts.[1] Since each reader is a unique reader, and since each reading of a creative text is a unique reading, there are new ways to view the concept of reading in quantum poetics. In quantum physics, an observer or measurement influences what is observed by changing it. Can reading be seen as an observation or a measurement of a text that is subject to the properties of quantum theory?

In the Copenhagen interpretation of quantum physics, it is at the moment of observation that an object being observed comes into existence. Before the subatomic particles of an object are observed, they exist as all possible configurations in a superposition of their quantum states. In quantum theory, the observer is not a static subject position, just as a reader is not a static subject position in reader-response theory and L=A=N=G=U=A=G=E poetry. Since what is observed is based on the position in space and time of the observer, or the reader, that which is being observed—the particle or text—is not considered to have an independent existence in quantum theory. Existence itself is a mutable concept in quantum physics, which brings into question why reality is so often treated across cultures and disciplines of human inquiry as absolute.

Physics of the Impossible

Every poem asks that the reader read in a new way according to the poetic logic of the poem. The poetic logic of a poem is partly expressed by how the blank space interacts with the text. In poems that use the literary device of erasure, where words or letters are erased or occluded in textual settings where we see the erasure in action, discerning readers will consider the reason for the erasure. They may explore the erasure in relation to what is not erased, the thematic significance of the erasure, and the impact that the erasure has on the poem. Erasure can be viewed as a symbol for silence, a gesture for not understanding, or a representation of speech being blocked. Erasure, as a literary device, foregrounds the spacetime of the page through the interaction of text with the occluded spaces of a poem.

Erasure is one literary device used by poet M. NourbeSe Philip in her book-length poem *Zong!* (2008), named after the African slave ship Zong, whose approximately 150 slaves, considered cargo, were murdered by drowning so that the ship's owners could collect insurance money. *Zong!*, written with the words from the legal decision where the insurance money was being sought, uses erasure to enact the atrocity of the erased lives of the slaves. Interacting with the spacetime on the page, the erasure in *Zong!* foregrounds visibility, bringing the atrocity into view. The erasure also serves the book's thematic and formal concerns of telling a story that cannot be told, discussed by Philip in the notes at the end of the book.[1]

In quantum poetics, poetic language is both a conceptual and material construct that not only reflects but forges physical reality. Poems are organized objects of this material language, making what was once invisible visible, similar to how erasure functions in *Zong!*. Poems, as material objects in the physical universe, are capable of altering our experience with thinking in ways that cannot otherwise be achieved, since thinking happens through language.

40 | THE IMAGINARY PRESENT

If a poem could exist on a rocket ship traveling at the speed of light where, in Albert Einstein's theory of relativity, space compresses, mass increases, and time slows, what kind of poem might it be? Michio Kaku, in *Physics of the Impossible*, says that according to Albert Einstein's theory of general relativity, profound distortions of spacetime would have to occur in a universe where the speed of light is constant.[2] In *Zong!*, the arrangements of text units inhabit aspects of Einstein's universe. The blank space in the poem compresses in relation to the text units like the space in Einstein's rocket ship traveling at the speed of light, a phenomenon known as time dilation in relativity. The broken words and erasures in the poem create the impression of time slowing amid the compression of space, hauntingly enacting the experience of drowning by those on the slave ship. Mass or matter increases through the physical elongation of text units in the poem, where words and phrases are not only erased but broken and stretched. However, unlike in relativity, the speed of light in *Zong!* is not constant. In contrast to visually normative poems situated in a Newtonian universe, where the passage of time is assumed to be uniform, *Zong!* is traveling through a universe where spacetime itself can contract and expand.

Philip told me that one of the formal constraints she used in the book is to never place text units directly below other text units so that there would always be space (and thus time) above each text unit, symbolizing the way that poetry can represent, in her words, "a moving toward."[3] Poetry needs space and time to move and to be "a moving toward."

In this quantum poetical reading of *Zong!*, the poem is inhabiting aspects of general relativity and special relativity. If a reader thinks of a page of poetry as a two-dimensional representation of the universe, in *Zong!*, as in relativity, space is not empty and matter does not inertly move through space. Matter tells spacetime how to warp the spacetime in its vicinity, and warped spacetime tells matter how to behave. The way that matter and spacetime interact in relativity, as well as how wormholes are conceived by Einstein, are useful for developing thought experiments in quantum poetics. Kaku notes that in Einstein's universe, the shortest distance between two points is not a straight line; if we curled a sheet of paper until two points touched, then the shortest distance between two points is a wormhole.[4]

By visually enacting its subject matter like a curled piece of paper

Physics of the Impossible | 41

representing a wormhole in Einstein's universe, *Zong!* functions as a wormhole between the Zong massacre in 1781 and the reader today. This wormhole invites more nuanced forms of remembrance and sorrow for those murdered. It also demands more outrage over racism, exploitation, and the ongoing impacts of the transatlantic slave trade. Is this wormhole that *Zong!* makes material or figurative? That depends on the poetics—and the physics—of the reader.

The Poetry Accelerator

Upon meeting poet Christian Bök before his poetry reading in Boulder, Colorado, I mentioned that his Xenotext experiment, where he was encoding a poem into a live bacterium to create an archive that might outlive humans, inspired me to imagine encoding a poem into a proton that could be sent through the Large Hadron Collider, the high-energy particle accelerator that had recently launched at CERN.

I knew that Bök was working with a MacArthur Fellow specializing in biocomplexity and informatics to help him in his poetry-bacterium synthesis. *What resources!* I oohed and awed. *A fleet of scientists!* I embellished. I considered the possibilities of someday collaborating with a particle physicist to make my own scenario feasible. *Do you know how you will you encode the poem into the proton?* Christian asked me. I replied, *No. How are you encoding the poem into the bacterium? Are you creating a cipher of some kind?* He began explaining that, yes, he's creating a cipher, and just when he got to the part about protein synthesis—poems and protein synthesis!—we were interrupted.[1] No matter, I shrugged, because the transformational aspect of the encounter was in seeing that to develop and expose the literary dimensions of science, and the scientific dimensions of literature, as Bök and others like Eduardo Kac were doing, the poet must become a kind of scientist, a kind of cipher.

Bök's Oulipian and conceptual sound experiments, with all their cross-wiring alien tech & reflexive virtuoso & 'pataphysical self-discipline & hypnotic modems, imagine the poetic project as a vast laboratory, one that invents rather than merely applies linguistic and scientific methods—and by vast, I mean in spacetime, as is evidenced by his *Xenotext*'s reach into its mutable borders. Bernard Carr's *Universe or Multiverse* (2007) notes that primitive humans were aware of scales from miles to mountains, eighteenth-century humans were aware of scales from bacteria to the solar system, and twentieth-century humans were aware of scales from atomic nuclei to distant galaxies.[2] After experiencing Bök's incantatory poetry reading, where I was moved—to tears!—and thinking about another uncanny performance of creative, rhythmic dimension, a concert by the musical groups *Melvins* and the *Butthole Surfers* the following night—I kept asking: What new scales do our poems propose?

The Poetics of Scale

When astrophysicists say that the universe is expanding, they mean that according to evidence from scientific discoveries, spacetime is expanding at an accelerating rate, which is making the known universe bigger. The acceleration of the expanding universe in the field of astrophysics describes how the spacetime between large forms of matter in the universe, such as galaxies, is increasing. One major theory as to why spacetime is increasing is because of dark energy, which is thought to change how gravity behaves at cosmological scales.

Instead of particles of matter coming together, bound by gravity, as they do inside of galaxies and on planetary bodies such as Earth, outside of galactic systems, dark energy acts upon matter as a repulsive force, moving matter from matter. Large objects of bound matter being moved from other large objects of bound matter in outer space creates more spacetime between these objects. When more spacetime is generated between large objects such as galaxies, the known universe expands by getting bigger. Scientists theorize that this is how the universe evolved to where it is now from a dimensionless point at the Big Bang.

Galaxies are thought to have evolved through varying mechanisms, including the supermassive black holes that many scientists think exist within each of their centers. Black holes are extreme environments within galaxies that absorb space, time, light, and energy. The scientific discovery of gravitational waves, created by two black holes that collided in the early universe after orbiting each other, verified a theory by Albert Einstein. He proposed that massive, accelerating objects in the universe, not yet named black holes, that orbit each other could disrupt spacetime in such a way that spacetime would ripple in waves, moving away from the source of the disruption in all directions. Some of these waves of spacetime passed through Earth when scientists were finally able to detect them with scientific experiments.

Let's apply these scientific discoveries and conceptual frameworks about our universe to poetry in a thought experiment using quantum poetics. First, we should say the obvious, that poetry is made of language, which is made by humans who live in a universe. Humanity is not separate from nature but part of nature, just as a galaxy is nature and spacetime is nature. Differences exist between a human, a galaxy, and spacetime, from material composition to the scales of the universe in which each can interact, but all three phenomena are part of the universe's larger environment, what we call nature. These foundational acknowledgments, that nature exists at varying scales of physical reality, and that everything defined as the universe is a part of it, were necessary as I first began thinking about physics in relation to the literary arts.

Next, if we imagine a poem as a planet, then as a galaxy, and then as a universe, we can experiment with how natural phenomena such as space, time, and gravity might interact with poetic language in different settings. In earlier chapters of this book, I started to explore how space and time can interact with a poem, acting to slow and speed pacing, for example. I also explored how gravity might be strong in the work of writers such as Gertrude Stein, who created density using repetitions of language. Similarly, gravity can be seen as weak in a poem made of detached phrasing or in an artwork by Chagall that evokes weightlessness. All of these ways that space, time, and gravity might behave in a poem or artwork treat the poem or artwork as a planet with its own laws of physics unique to its environment.

Let's scale up. How might space, time, and gravity work in a poem that is a galaxy? The shape of the galaxy would need to be determined. Will it be elliptical, a barred spiral like the Milky Way, or something else? If our poem is a barred spiral galaxy, we could use spacetime to evoke our poem's shape. We could use a strong gravity, one that is even stronger than what was used by Stein, to suggest the intense compression of space, time, and light in the black hole at our poem's center. We could write a Sun into space, shining light into our poem.

What if the poem we are writing is a universe? Will the poem be a high-gravity universe or low-gravity universe like our universe is theorized to be? If it's a high-gravity universe, our poem might not be our universe but another universe within the multiverse. In a high-gravity universe that is a poem, everything would be so compressed by gravity

46 | THE IMAGINARY PRESENT

that the poem could be a black hole. What kind of poem would our poem be if it was a black hole?

Let's scale down, way down to the subatomic world of quantum theory. Instead of our poem being a universe, a galaxy, or a planet, let's imagine that our poem is a subatomic particle in quantum superposition, existing in all possible configurations at once. Its spacetime would contain all possible spacetimes. What if our poem was not a subatomic particle but a quantum dimension that could access the energy limit in our universe known as the Planck scale? Beyond the Planck scale, the laws of physics break down. But at the Planck scale, all the current questions that scientists have about the universe would be answered, since the universe's most intricate properties would be revealed. What kind of poem could be invented to evoke this threshold at the Planck scale? What kind of poem could be this threshold?

Just Schrödinger the Text!

Werner Heisenberg's matrix mechanics in quantum theory was challenged by Erwin Schrödinger in the latter's formulation of the famous thought experiment, Schrödinger's Cat. The thought experiment attempts to demonstrate that Heisenberg's approach to quantum theory breaks down at other scales of matter beyond the subatomic.

In the thought experiment, a cat, sealed in a box, is both alive and dead at the same time until it is observed when the box is opened. Inside the box, the cat exists in a quantum superposition of life and death until an observer opens the box, measuring whether the cat is alive or dead, at which point the cat becomes either alive or dead. Schrödinger used the thought experiment to show how a cat being alive and dead at the same time, before it is observed, fails the standards of classical logic. Heisenberg, however, was a few steps ahead of Schrödinger.

Not only is the measurement of radiation emitted from an atom impossible without ambiguity, Heisenberg demonstrated, measurement cannot define an observed system in relation to the observer's apparatus.[1] In other words, an observation of the cat cannot define the cat as certainly dead or alive. The reason is that the observer is a part of the quantum system of what is being observed, which, in Schrödinger's thought experiment, is the cat in the box. The observer, by making the observation, changes the cat's state as it appears to the observer. People are often incredulous about this aspect of quantum theory, because it goes against so much of what we often assume about existence. In the scientific experiment known as the double-slit experiment, a cornerstone of quantum theory, an observer or measurement changes what is observed or measured through the action of observation or measurement.

I recently taught an undergraduate special topics course in creative writing called Space, Time, Light that engaged literary and scientific treat-

48 | THE IMAGINARY PRESENT

ments of these three phenomena. For one class, the chair of the physics department at my university, physicist Daniel Kim-Shapiro, performed the double-slit experiment for my students using a simple laser beam and projector that emulated the experiment with a plate pierced by two parallel slits. The experiment shows that light can be both a wave and a particle at the same time, which led to a fundamental principle in quantum theory known as wave-particle duality. Just as Schrödinger's cat can be both alive and dead at the same time inside the box, and the cat becomes defined as either alive or dead when observed, light becomes defined as either a wave or a particle when it is measured. After the double-slit experiment was performed and explained by our visiting physicist, one of the students said, *Okay! If a tree falls in the forest, does it make a sound?* Our visiting physicist said, *Well, according to quantum theory, we can't say that there is a tree.*[2]

Schrödinger's objections to quantum theory assume that the observer does not influence that cat's state upon opening the box. But according to Heisenberg, "It is not possible to decide, other than arbitrarily, what objects are to be considered as part of the observed system and what as part of the observer's apparatus."[3] In other words, the apparatus measuring whether the cat is alive or dead upon opening the sealed box—the human observer in the double-slit experiment—is part of the experiment. Heisenberg applies quantum theory to other scales of material reality beyond the subatomic to present "the indeterminateness of the picture of the process."[4] Not only is the quantum cat indeterminate, the process of observing the cat is too. While in relativity the universe is thought to be deterministic, in quantum theory the universe is thought to be indeterminate, an idea that often unsettles people. However, as a poet, I feel at ease with the idea that the universe is indeterminate. Poetry is indeterminate.

> both alive and dead
> at the same time,
> the n-dimensional cat
> in its mythic box
> is inside another
> box called a room,
> and if each room

Just Schrödinger the Text! | 49

> *contains all*
> *possible rooms, and*
> *if some rooms*
> *are cubes in three*
> *dimensions, this*
> *poem, in superposition,*
> *is a tesseract of*
> *overlapping cubes*
> *inside a room we call*
> *a page, one we*
> *keep entering and*
> *leaving by reading*
> *and writing it*

Schrödinger and Heisenberg developed different mathematics for quantum theory, with Heisenberg's coming first but Schrödinger's initially championed.[5] The mathematics of each theory give nearly equivalent results. Schrödinger developed wave mechanics, where particles are thought to move by waves that guide them, while Heisenberg developed matrix mechanics, where particles in superposition move by a quantum jump.

Another difference between the two mathematics is that Heisenberg developed his using matrices, grids that are added and multiplied in patterns. Matrices had not been previously used in this exact manner in physics. The matrix form of matrix mechanics is similar to an invented literary form that might be found in poetry, in that Heisenberg had to develop a new scientific form to yield new content. While classical mechanics and wave mechanics are more traditional mathematics used in physics, matrix mechanics was different in that it challenged the conventions of physics by creating an abstract mathematics to represent mechanical properties of the atom such as position, velocity, and momentum. In this way, matrix mechanics is a form of poiesis, the Ancient Greek word for "making." Poets, like physicists, also invent forms for their content.

Schrödinger's wave mechanics was the mechanics initially embraced by the status quo in physics because of its familiar mathematics and visualizability.[6] While wave mechanics and Heisenberg's matrix mechanics produced equivalent results, Schrödinger argued that his theory was

50 | THE IMAGINARY PRESENT

superior because it rejected the claim that subatomic particles move by quantum jump, outside of the law of deterministic causality or cause and effect.[7] Soon after Schrödinger said this, Heisenberg wrote a letter to his friend, physicist Wolfgang Pauli, which later became published as an article publicly presenting the uncertainty principle. The letter to Pauli showed how the uncertainty principle explained experimental data.[8]

Schrödinger said that he was repelled by Heisenberg's matrix mechanics because of its difficult mathematics and lack of visualizability.[9] In addition to the problem of abstraction in Heisenberg's matrix mechanics, Schrödinger, like Albert Einstein, could not accept the seemingly paradoxical nature of the quantum jump, in which subatomic particles move outside of cause and effect.[10] While Heisenberg's matrix mechanics was eventually embraced by physics and is used today, when Heisenberg first proposed it as a new mathematics for quantum theory, his peers had a difficult time understanding it.[11] The story of Schrödinger and Heisenberg speaks to how new ideas, including scientific ideas, that depend on poetic thinking can radically challenge existing paradigms in a world where realism and classical logic reign.

Poetry and Science

The Two Most Incompatible Disciplines

Let's summarize what this book has proposed so far. Science and poetry have nothing in common. Science deals only in fact, truth, and knowledge. Poetry deals only in emotion, experience, and wonder. Science is a quest for wisdom, poetry is a quest. Science is analytical. Poetry is intuitive. Science is real. Poetry is not real. Poetry is an art. Science is an art. Poetry is political. Poetry is useful because it persuades. Science is never political, but sometimes it persuades. Science is sometimes political, especially with climate change and evolution. Poetry solves social problems while science solves mathematical problems. Poetry rights problems. Poetry is personal. My poetry is about me, but your science isn't about you.

Science is used to heal people. Poetry is used to heal people. Poetry cannot be used to kill people. Sometimes science is used to kill people. There are poetry wars and science wars. Nobody ever died because of a poem unless the poem was propaganda. That's a fact, and poetry deals in fact, truth, and knowledge. Science is objective, while poetry is subjective. Poetry is all about its subject. Science is all about its object. Scientists observe nature. Poets observe nature. Poetry instructs and inspires. Poetry always has a point. Poetry must point us to what is truthful and beautiful. Science can point us only to truth, but beauty matters to scientists.

In *The Wizard of Oz*, poetry is the con man behind the curtain who claims to be the wizard, and science is what makes the wizard seem powerful. Science challenges religious authority. Poetry challenges religious authority. Poetry is good. Science is good. When science creates atomic weapons, science is bad. When poetry is bad, we just mean aesthetically.

Science gets a bad rap. Poetry gets a bad rap. Poetry is ignored. Science

51

52 | THE IMAGINARY PRESENT

is ignored. Science is attacked by those who do not believe in climate change or evolution. Poetry is attacked by those who see it as confusing or irrelevant. Science is attacked by those with corporate interests when science gets in the way of profit. Poetry is attacked by poets who champion a specific approach to poetry. Science and profit do not mix. Poetry and profit do not mix. Science can make money. Poetry cannot make money. Poetry can make a little money.

Poetry should be about beauty or trauma. Science is never about beauty or trauma. Science is mostly about data. Poetry is all about data in conceptual poetry. Poetry is about not only data but the appropriation of data in conceptual poetry. Poetry is so data it is Dada! Poetry is so Dada it can be offensive. Science is never Dada and never offensive. Science is slightly Dada in superstring theory but never offensive. Science is offensive only to those who oppose it. Poetry is offensive only to those who oppose it. Science is policed for inaccuracies, and poetry is policed for offense. The police for science and the police for poetry wear different uniforms.

Scientists dream but do not use their dreams to conduct science. Science deals in fact, truth, and knowledge. Dreams don't matter in science because science is real. Dreams are not real. Poets do all the dreaming. Poets use dreams to make poetry. Dreams matter in poetry because reality is only somewhat real.

You cannot fix a broken bone with a poem. You cannot fix a broken heart with science. Poetry and science should fix things like hearts and bones. Poetry should be done for its own sake. Science should be done for its own sake. Science imagines the unimaginable and tests it with expensive equipment. Poetry imagines the unimaginable and only needs paper, pencils, and laptops. Poetry needs time, which is expensive. Poetry needs audiences. Science needs funding. Poetry needs funding, but unlike science, poetry can be compromised with too much funding. Poetry does not get better with money. Poetry can get a little better with money. Science gets better with money. Just look at the Large Hadron Collider.

Poetry is all about the materiality of language. Science is never about the materiality of language. Poetry is sincere and satiric. Science is sincere but never satiric. Poetry can be sincere and satiric at the same time, like right now. Science is only sincere.

Science is biased in its questions. Poetry is sometimes biased. Poetry is only biased when the poet is biased. Science is only biased when the scientist is biased. Science is written in the language of mathematics. Poetry is a translation of ordinary language into creative thinking. Poetry and science are all about language. Poetry and science are all about translation. Poetry is about community. Poetry communities are supportive. Science communities are supportive. Poetry communities are ruthless. Science communities are ruthless. There is mediocrity in poetry and mediocrity in science. Only the most conservative ideas in poetry are rewarded. Only the most conservative ideas in science are rewarded. Sometimes radical questions are rewarded in poetry. Sometimes radical questions are rewarded in science. Poets should ask: What is the physics of my poem? Physicists should ask: What are the poetics of my physics?

It is fine to be a poet and not understand science. Poetry is not about knowledge. Poetry is about experience. Poetry is not about experience. Poetry is about transcendence. Poetry is not about transcendence. Poetry is about inquiry. Poetry is not about inquiry. Poetry is about creativity. Poetry is not about creativity. Poetry is about history. Poetry is good only when it teaches history. Poetry should teach things. Poetry should not have to teach things. Poetry should evoke things. Science should teach things, but not history.

Poetry is all about play and surprise. Poetry's emphasis on play makes it frivolous. Poets should not be frivolous. Poetry is a vehicle for transformation. Poetry is always a vehicle for something. Poets drive Toyotas and Priuses; scientists, Teslas. Sometimes poets drive Teslas. Scientists should be serious but also artistic. Science should never be frivolous. Poets should be frivolous. There are rules for poetry, and there are rules for science. KNOW THE RULES, AND DON'T BREAK THEM. When breaking the rules in poetry and science, know why. Always know why you are breaking the rules. This is the first rule about breaking rules. Never break rules for the sake of breaking rules. That is the second rule about breaking rules.

Poets should write what they know. Physicists should only believe what they can see. If poets cannot suspend their belief in what they see, who can? Physicists, that's who!

Spin the Kaleidoscope

A dramatic sky of dark clouds swirled above me and the filmmaker and artist David Blair as we stood near the top of the Robert C. Byrd Green Bank Telescope (GBT), the world's largest steerable radio telescope. Like the other telescopes at the National Radio Astronomy Observatory in West Virginia, the GBT reads incoming radio signals from outer space. In 1960, astronomer Frank D. Drake was the first to search for interstellar radio transmissions at the observatory, famously pioneering decades of experiments known as SETI (Search for Extraterrestrial Life), which continue to this day.

The next day the weather was much sunnier. In protective red safety helmets, and after taking the freight elevator once again to near the top of the telescope with a staff member, we were surrounded by the other telescopes and different mountain ranges in the distance. The GBT is known for detecting cosmological phenomena, including the Ophiuchus Superbubble, a cavity in our solar system hundreds of light-years across with a dense shell made of cooled, interstellar gas.[1] We were standing on one of humanity's most powerful eyes that sees spacetime in light-years. Our goal that day was to shoot footage for David's film project, with both of us to act as a version of the main character, Jacob Maker. This character, a multiphasic, first-person narrator, is a weapons system simulator technician, beekeeper, and salesperson of telepathic films in Alamogordo, New Mexico. Alamogordo is the site of Trinity, the world's first test of the atomic weapon resulting from the Manhattan Project, 210 miles south of Los Alamos.

The project we were shooting was *The Telepathic Motion Picture of THE LOST TRIBES*, a twenty-six-season, twenty-six-episode-per-season ongoing video-television series by David, a sequel to his 1991 cult feature film *Wax or the Discovery of Television Among the Bees* (1991), which includes a cameo by

54

William S. Burroughs. *Wax* was the first film streamed on the Internet. The online, hypermedia version of the film, WAXWEB (1994), was one of the first artist projects on the Internet. As the antiwar story unfolds, Jacob Maker, played mainly by David but occasionally by others like me, travels from the recognizable world of Alamogordo to new dimensions of space and time, each composed by a language of animated glyphs. The projects combine 3D and other animation, found footage, live action, and spoken story.[2]

On the telescope during the second day of our visit, David and I were each in our beekeeper uniforms as Jacob Maker. A few weeks earlier, at the Emily Dickinson House in Massachusetts, I had played Jacob Maker as Emily Dickinson playing Jacob Maker. Our beekeeper suits and veils resembled space-suits, which is appropriate since Jacob Maker is a traveler of spacetime. The goal of my performance that day, David directed me, was to look out from the edge of the telescope as Jacob Maker and slowly scan the horizon.

As I scanned the horizon, I began to read it.

I asked myself if we could be read as the radio telescope was reading the incoming radio waves that were traveling at the speed of light. This would make the environment around the radio waves *all here* and *all then* to an observer sitting astride the radio waves. Human culture regularly emits radio signals through television broadcasts that theoretically could be detected by life-forms in outer space. What other signals do humans emit into outer space? I wondered.

After being filmed reading the horizon, I decided to dance like Jacob Maker dances in *Wax*. I spun around, slowly, twirling on top of the telescope. David was still filming. By spinning, I imagined emitting a signal from Jacob Maker into the cosmos that was a poem. I also thought about how physics uses the term "spin" to signify that elementary particles contain an intrinsic angular momentum. We—Jacob Maker and me, and David Blair as Jacob Maker as David Blair—we were a novel alphabet, intrinsically composed of angular momentum, I mused. Our spinning made a poetic current through which our glyph-bodies could travel.

If radio telescopes, in reading radio waves from the cosmos, are readers of the cosmos, radio waves are languages, I speculated. We can imagine the Ophiuchus Superbubble as a cosmological poem read by the GBT. What material phenomena within the uncharted realms of physical reality might read the poem that is written in the novel alphabet that Jacob Maker spins?

Poetry and the Fourth Dimension

In *Mad Science in Imperial City* (2005), poet and former mechanical engineer Shanxing Wang asks a question about point of view in literature that suggests a new way of thinking about spacetime: "Is there a fourth-person narration?"[1] In conventional storytelling, narrative point of view, or how a story is told, often uses one of three perspectives: first-person point of view, told by an "I"; second-person point of view, told by a narrator using "you"; and third-person point of view, told by a "she," "he," or "they." Wang's question about fourth-person narrative point of view invites us to consider the fourth dimension, where the three dimensions of space intersect with the dimension of time, in relation to how perspective is managed by authors in literature. His question also suggests there may be narrative points of view beyond four dimensions, evoking the higher dimensions theorized in superstring theory in physics.

In quantum poetics, fourth-person narrative point of view can be seen in Virginia Woolf's *The Waves* (1931), where first-person point-of-view monologues from six characters are framed by italicized introductions to each chapter. These chapter-introductions are in third-person, omniscient point of view, where an unnamed narrator sees everything. They describe, incrementally, the sun rising and setting over the sea during one complete day.

The chapter-introductions swell against the elongated passages of time that follow the six lives of the characters from childhood through adulthood. Each character's first-person point-of-view monologue is spoken in present tense. The compression of time in the chapter-introductions that describe the rising and setting sun in its different stages throughout the day, and the expansion of time in the primary narrative told by each monologue, collide in a new narrative spacetime. By adopting a similar tone and cadence, the monologues suggest that consciousness is

Poetry and the Fourth Dimension | 57

both an individual and collective construct. Individual selfhood in *The Waves* is expanded through the varied immediacies of perception that are expressed by each character, existing as a singular whole in the collective medium of the story.

It is no surprise that Woolf thought of this book, her last, not as a novel but a "play-poem."[2] The book challenges expectations that readers have of narrative form through its self-reflexive formal structures, where the characters communicate plot events and concerns while metafictionally addressing language, poetry, and storytelling. This hyperdimensional literary form, like the fourth dimension in physics, operates as a spatiotemporal marker, an *Imaginary Present*, of a relative present tense that contains both the past and the future. Through its fourth-person narrative point of view, expressed in the relationship of the monologues to the descriptions of the rising and setting sun, *The Waves* subverts its conditions as a book, a three-dimensional object, by investigating its own materiality in fourth-dimensional spacetime.

Scientists largely agree that approximately ninety-six percent of the known universe consists of invisible dark matter and dark energy, yet we often participate in consensus reality as if reality can be seen. The fourth-person narrative point of view in *The Waves* argues that consciousness operates in many places at the same time. As part of the multiverse, the theory in physics that our universe is one of many universes, quantum poetics suggests that consciousness is unbound by the conventions of space and time as conceived in classical physics, moving toward novelty through art such as poetry, which equips the invisible universe to see us so that we might, in turn, see it. This seeing is not only scientific observation but artistic perception, much like a viewer sees Wonder Woman's invisible jet as a cartoon on television while ignoring the dotted outline that is meant to evoke it. Using both rational and creative thinking, the viewer simultaneously perceives Wonder Woman's jet as both visible and invisible.

Literary novelty, as in texts such as *The Waves*, is a revolutionary action toward fundamental change and reform. Reading and writing poetry and play-poems brings creative complexity to our rational thinking. They also make us more receptive to novelty in our lived experience. Practices like poetry, which is an activity of thinking and perception, is part of an evolutionary process toward novelty. Innovative art operates on different

58 | THE IMAGINARY PRESENT

frequencies from mainstream culture, like invisible radio waves traveling at the speed of light, sometimes registering as alien languages to those who don't, or refuse to, encounter them.

Leonard Shlain, in *Art & Physics*, argues that breakthroughs in the natural sciences and the visual arts have happened close together throughout history. How does a breakthrough in science, such as relativity, happen without direct connection to a similar breakthrough in art, such as cubism, in a universe where spacetime is measured against observers? We can imagine Gertrude Stein asking: *The question is this, Which came which, the chicken or the chicken. This question and the egg of course.* If the universe consists of dimensions beyond four, language also is operating beyond four dimensions. Was Gertrude Stein writing at the speed of light?

In geometry, zero dimension can be represented by a point on a piece of paper, one dimension by a line, and two dimensions by a plane, such as a square. The third dimension, which adds depth, is the dimension in which everyday objects exist. On paper with a two-dimensional outward face, three dimensions can be projected by drawing a cube. Scientists employ projection in more complex ways using lower-dimensional planes to conceptualize higher dimensions. The fourth dimension, which is the three dimensions of space and the dimension of time joined in one manifold, can be projected as a tesseract, which renders spacetime at or beyond four dimensions. *The Waves*, by way of its fourth-person narration, is a projection of the fourth dimension or more in the three dimensions of itself as a book.

The People of the Fifth Dimension

In superstring theory, physicists theorize that there are dimensions beyond the four of spacetime. Poet, artist, and scholar Charles "Chuck" Stein has suggested that a consciousness in the fifth dimension could time travel by moving freely between the three spatial states in the fourth dimension of ordinary spacetime.[1] Chuck makes elaborate ink drawings using images of tesseracts, mathematical depictions of four or more spacetime dimensions. The tesseracts are sometimes joined with Necker cubes, two-dimensional images that act as optical illusions by appearing to have surfaces inside and outside the images. The Fluxus artist Henry Flynt used Necker cubes and inspired Chuck to incorporate them into his drawings, he told me. The tesseracts and Necker cubes make his drawings appear to shift orientations.[2]

Chuck taught me how to draw tesseracts at a café in Red Hook, New York. He's a close friend of poet George Quasha and artist Susan Quasha, whom I was visiting in nearby Barrytown. I soon began a tesseract practice, frequently drawing them, and used them for a poetry project that involved hand-drawn and computer-rendered tesseracts. The first step to drawing a tesseract is to draw one three-dimensional cube overlapping another three-dimensional cube. Then the corresponding vertices between each cube must be attached. This is the challenging part of drawing a tesseract, because its higher dimensionality emerges as the vertices are being connected. It's difficult to keep seeing each corresponding vertex as the object gains visual complexity through the development of new faces. Within each face of a tesseract there is a distorted cube, further adding to the visual complexity.

I wanted to draw tesseracts because Chuck's drawings pulse. Some contain Roman letters and invented languages that he created. Some

59

60 | THE IMAGINARY PRESENT

include what look like atavistic symbols. Some look like hyperdimensional cities. Some have little stick people in them. The people represent "the people," he told me, and first appeared when he was active in the Occupy movement.[3]

The Positron Passport

Locality is an unproven axiom. The experiment has no end, and any beginning is a glitch. In the book's quantum jump, entanglement is where we left off. Before the clouds and white moth orchids were blurred as evidence of interactions. Between particles. Interrupting orchids reversing into fleshy clouds. From pictures that carry signals.

Among these temporal geographies we read the sky. In this window that constructs spacetime. The frame, a poetics, keeps adjusting its position. To include the poem inside and outside the frame as an afterimage of the frame's ongoing entrance.

Translating spacetime requires these conditions of everywhere. I use a line but mean a birdsong for my starting principle. In orbit around each syllable, a star machine brings heavy centers to heat. In a present that never was or will be as real as the modes of language that attempt to describe it.

> Inside these distances
> Unfolding a return to
> Like a belief we need
> Episodically in revolt

If the known universe is a bubble in the multiverse, its volume could be written in a liquescent alphabet where many worlds are within worlds in

s
su
sup
supe
super
superp
superpo
superpos
superposi
superposit
superpositi
superpositio
superposition
uperposition
perposition
erposition
rposition
position
osition
sition
ition
tion
ion
on
n

The manyworlds within worlds in superposition is a sound wave of a birdsong shaped like a leaf on a page. In the known universe, all matter, like a leaf, like a page, is made of atoms. Quantum theory describes the properties of these atoms. An atom is made of electrons spinning around a nucleus. An atomic nucleus is made of protons and neutrons, which are made of quarks and gluons. In superstring theory, quarks and gluons are connected by open and closed strings, one-dimensional membranes of energy embedded within two-dimensional surfaces of spacetime known as worldsheets.

Open strings are shaped like lines. Some connect to D-branes, membranes upon which each side of an open string can end. Closed strings are

The Positron Passport | 63

shaped like circles. In superstring theory, open and closed strings vibrate through the multiverse, the theorized collection of universes of which our known universe may be a part.

> *This line is an open string.*
> *Each side of the line ends*
> *not in blank space but on*
> *a D-brane, a membrane*
> *that interacts with gravity.*
> *Within galaxies, things with*
> *mass are brought together by*
> *gravity due to the curvature*
> *of spacetime. The o in open*
> *is a closed string: a circle*
> *made of infinite curves.*
> *Gravity pulls words down.*
> *This page is a worldsheet,*
> *a two-dimensional surface*
> *outside the experiment's*
> *framed windows through*
> *which this poem is read.*
> *This poem is a new window*
> *inside the framed windows,*
> *but one that has no image*
> *of the white moth orchids*
> *until now. By describing*
> *the lines, letters, page, and*
> *itself using superstring*
> *theory, this poem, a narrow*
> *window inside the framed*
> *windows that are inside the*
> *page, which is a worldsheet,*
> *contains the worldsheet*
> *inside its frame, the worlds*
> *and their sheets, and the*
> *letter s that they share.*

64 | THE IMAGINARY PRESENT

S is also for spacetime. In the early known universe, spacetime underwent a phase transition from one state to another. Empty space filled with an invisible Higgs energy field with which all particles interact to gain mass. The discovery of the Higgs field accompanied the discovery of the Higgs boson by the ATLAS and CMS detectors in the Large Hadron Collider (LHC) at CERN. The most powerful high-energy particle accelerator on Earth, the LHC collides protons in a circular, seventeen-mile tunnel under parts of Switzerland and France, recreating the early conditions of the universe so that physicists can study its underlying structure. Before the discovery of the Higgs boson, it was a hypothesized particle in the Standard Model of physics, a theoretical framework that aims to describe how matter interacts with fundamental forces. Other theoretical frameworks in physics include quantum theory, which describes matter at subatomic scales, and the theory of relativity, which describes matter at cosmological scales.

Quantum theory rejects the law of deterministic causality, known as cause and effect, and many ordinary intuitions of experience, where it is often assumed that observed objects are not influenced by observation. In quantum theory, the observer affects what is being observed or measured. Entangled quantum states of particles can influence each other over distances without physically interacting if they once had been in local proximity. These properties of quantum systems are understood to behave outside of classical notions of cause and effect. What is less understood is that they also behave outside of classical notions of language.

One difficulty of quantum theory is the way in which ordinary language does not suffice in describing its principles. In *Physics and Philosophy*, Werner Heisenberg emphasizes that ordinary language is inadequate in describing both cosmological and subatomic systems.[1] In discussing how space and time are newly conceived in the theory of relativity, he remarks, "No language existed in which one could speak consistently about the new situation. The ordinary language was based upon the old concepts of space and time. . . . Yet the experiments showed that the old concepts could not be applied everywhere."[2] A similar problem occurs in quantum theory, Heisenberg says: "The most difficult problem . . . concerning the use of the language arises in quantum theory. Here we have at first no simple guide for correlating the mathematical symbols with concepts of ordinary language . . . our common concepts cannot be applied to the structure of the atoms."[3] In describing how quantum theory challenges Newtonian classical mechanics, which relies on the axiom that observers can formulate laws about nature, Heisenberg gets us to question if reality can be observed directly: "We have to remember that what we observe is not nature in itself but nature exposed to our method of questioning."[4]

Quantum poetics asks: If poetry, because of its anarchic interaction with its environment, is a novel method of questioning that artistic language performs, what is nature when exposed to a method of questioning that is a poem, where the form and content of the question, through the creative action of the imagination, can quantum jump in any and all directions?

Two years after the LHC went operational at CERN, I published an essay-poem, "Quantum Poetics: Tripping Farther Down the Rabbit Hole" (2010) in *Critiphoria: A Journal of Poetry and Criticism*, that imagined encoding letters inside the protons that are collided in a particle accelerator. Nine years later, I was at CERN with the ATLAS experiment, collaborating with particle physicist James Beacham on how this thought experiment could be realized. Nine years earlier, I had imagined that the letters, which would comprise a poem, would collide with the protons near the speed of light, possibly forming a new poem the way proton collisions can discover new matter. The only way to read this new poem after the collision of the protons would be to interpret its interference patterns, its tracks and traces of movement, just like physicists do with the protons collided in the LHC. I thought of Emily Dickinson:

We met as Sparks—Diverging Flints
Sent various—scattered ways—[5]

In the particle accelerator, under the influence of clinamen, Lucretius's atomic swerve, where a spontaneous interruption of a straight path creates new matter by bending it toward other matter,[6] the letters like the protons in which they were encoded would deviate from their ordinarily straight paths, bent by the superconducting electromagnets within the circular tunnel. I imagined the circular tunnel containing this proton-poem as a closed string in superstring theory.

I first went to CERN to research particle physics. I was introduced

66 | THE IMAGINARY PRESENT

to scientists who work there by my sponsor, Juan José Gómez Cadenas, a specialist in astroparticle, nuclear, and high-energy physics who also writes poetry and fiction. One meeting he set up for me was with Gian Francesco Giudice, at the time the head of the Department of Theoretical Physics. Giudice works on collider and astroparticle physics, cosmology, Standard Model, and beyond Standard Model phenomenology. According to Giudice, at 126 gigaelectronvolts, the Higgs field has the correct value to keep the known universe at the edge of another phase transition into a second, denser state of the Higgs field. However, because of the uncertainty principle in quantum theory, even if there is a barrier between these two Higgs states, there is a nonzero probability of an energy transfer occurring from the known universe to the second, denser Higgs field.[7] In mathematics, every event is given a probability between zero and one, where zero indicates the impossibility of the event and one indicates certainty. The energy transfer between the two Higgs states is impossible in classical mechanics. But in quantum mechanics it could happen through the action of what is known as quantum tunnelling, where subatomic particles, having both particle and wave-like behavior, a condition called "wave-particle duality," would borrow energy from their surroundings to jump the barrier between the two Higgs states, resulting in an exchange of energy between the known universe and the second, denser Higgs field.

Locality is an unproven axiom.

If quantum theory predicts that there is a small but nonzero probability, which means a certainty, that objects without the energy to overcome a barrier will appear on the other side, the definition of a barrier is a scalable concept. In quantum theory and poetry, barriers are overcome when potential matter borrows energy from its environment to perform a quantum jump, a movement theorized by the uncertainty principle, where position changes momentum and momentum changes position. What if entangled quantum states of particles that had once been near each other but are now separated across distance, performing instantaneous exchanges of information, are quantum tunnelling through spacetime? Locality is not only an unproven axiom, an assumption that guides classical logic, it transcends the conceptual, spatiotemporal barriers of classical mechanics and classical language, the language of ordinary prose.

what is the sound
      just before

a bird sings?   *near the power*

          station adorning
      the moving planet
generating
      machine intelligence
            across skylines,
where cloud orchids
            buffer
                  the lyric effect of words
            far above
                  the radio telescopes
                        over there
                        that receive
      the dream data
                  from where we take
                        our sleep,
                  a world-
                        sheet
                  where
            the gravitational
                  pull
                        on the page
      laces letters
in the mind,
            a field of energy
      giving
                  mass
                        to
                  particles
                  and
                        poems

68 | THE IMAGINARY PRESENT

Giudice and I had discussed the high-resonance anomaly that was detected by the LHC a few months earlier, a possible new particle not predicted by the Standard Model. Later, the anomaly was proven to not be a particle. But when we spoke, there was the exciting possibility that the anomaly was a newly discovered particle like the Higgs boson. He told me about the paper he had just cowritten that invented a theoretical framework in which this new particle could exist. I was curious if the anomaly could be the graviton, the theorized subatomic particle for gravity and the only elementary particle in the Standard Model that had not yet been proven to exist through experimental verification. The discovery of the graviton would lead to breakthroughs that could reconcile quantum theory with relativity. Giudice explained that the anomaly could be a graviton, a mistake, or something else.

His work in describing a new theoretical framework for the existence of the anomaly, he said, is like finding a tiny bone from one dinosaur that might not even be a bone and then trying to reconstruct the bodies of all dinosaurs.[8] Discussing his analogy that explains how the anomaly, if it was a new particle, would provoke the remapping of physics itself, we talked about how scientists, like poets, use literary devices to translate ideas from one domain to another. I explained that just as there are theoretical frameworks in physics, and some of these frameworks are accepted while others are challenged or rejected, there are theoretical frameworks, known as poetics, that operate in literature. In quantum poetics, I said, I consider poetry and science in union. While quantum poetics draws from conventional logic, poetic logic is also treated as a legitimate mode of investigation. Importantly, I said, quantum poetics makes efforts to avoid co-opting science for predetermined conclusions, but it also dares to speculate.

Giudice told me the story of how he and his collaborators named the potential new particle *digamma*, since, at 756 gigaelectronvolts, it is about six units the mass of the Higgs boson. The story of the potential particle's name, referenced in a footnote in the cowritten paper that he later sent me, describes how *digamma* is double gamma, the third letter of the archaic Greek alphabet. Descriptive of the letter's original shape, *digamma* is an ancestor of the Latin letter *f* that stood for the Phoenician letter *wāw*, the *w* sound in English. The *digamma* letter was present in Linear B Mycenean Greek and Æolic Greek but later disappeared from Classical Greek,

The Positron Passport | 69

likely before the seventh century BC. It remained in use as a symbol for the number six, because it occupies the sixth place in the Greek alphabet. In Byzantine times it was known as *episēmon*, and since the Middle Ages it became known in Greek as *stigma*, which means "sign," "mark," or "punctuation." Giudice said that the historical precedent of the disappearance of the letter *f* is a reminder that caution is necessary, that the anomaly might not be a newly discovered particle after all, and that the likelihood of a possible discovery might disappear.[9]

I said that should the anomaly be proven to be a new particle I would write a sestina for it. I explained how a sestina, with its repeating end words in a set pattern and six stanzas of six lines each with a seventh stanza of three lines containing all the end words, would speak to the emphasis on the number six in the *digamma*'s name. The end words also rhythmically act as a sign of closure emphasized even in enjambments, where lines grammatically continue past a line break, through their set repetitions. My end words for the sestina, I later thought, would all start with the letter *w*, an homage to the *w* sound written as *wāw*, the Phoenician letter described by the Latin letter *f*, the ancestor of *digamma*, descriptive of the letter's original shape:

> *words,*
> > *worlds,*
> *why,*
> > *window,*
> *wave,*

write. All but one of the end words, write, would start with the sound, *wāw*, bringing emphasis to the break in pattern. Like clinamen, which spontaneously quantum jumps from an established path, it would be the word write that swerved in my sestina.

On the campus of CERN, a large statue of Nataraja Shiva, the male Hindu god who ecstatically dances the universe into a cycle of existence and extinction, appears in a small courtyard square surrounded by buildings. The statue, a gift from India's Department of Atomic Energy, looks toward the LHC in the far distance, expressing the power of both creativity and destruction in Shakti, the life force. According to the commem-

70 | THE IMAGINARY PRESENT

orative plaque near the statue, the universe is an act of creation, sparked by the vibration of a drum held by one of Shiva's hands. An open hand grants freedom from fear, offering protection. The fire in another hand dissolves the universe. A leg stomps a dwarf, who represents ignorance. The aureole around Shiva represents the cosmos revolving in perpetual motion. At dark, Shiva lights up. Visitors of CERN stay at simple hotels near the statue, and each night of my stay during this visit, diagonally across from me, a massive shadow from the statue reflected on a building, creating two dancing Shivas, the statue and its shadow. Since binaries are not quantum, I began looking for the third Shiva.

The campus of CERN is dotted with artworks, some sculptures of decommissioned particle physics technology. One piece displays a long tube that looks like a slide on a playground. Another resembles a human-inspired robot. At the Globe of Science and Innovation, a museum and performance space, I saw the world's first computer server that was created at CERN, a legendary device among Internet archeologists. A metal sculpture outside the globe contains the names of physicists, cultures, and scientific discoveries written in different typographies and languages on a massive swath of ribboning, curved metal. During my first visit to CERN, on a cloudy day about to storm, the sculpture was largely in shadow except for Einstein's equation for the speed of light, lit up brightly by a single beam.

After my meeting with CERN's general director, physicist Fabiola Gianotti, she asked her staff to arrange a tour for me of the Antiproton Decelerator, known as the Antimatter Factory, with its director, physicist Michael Doser, who also explores connections between science and art. He showed me international collaborations studying antimatter, including the Antihydrogen Laser Physics Apparatus (ALPHA) experiment, which later observed the light spectrum of antimatter for the first time.[10] On a different day, I saw the ATLAS control room, recognizable from the documentary film *Particle Fever* (2013), about the discovery of the Higgs boson. During my second visit to CERN, while the LHC was offline, I went underground to the ATLAS and CMS detectors, where the particle collisions occur. The next day, I was with James Beacham in front of the two New Small Wheels, the upgrades being made to ATLAS that resemble giant, blue wheel-flowers. It was there that I mentioned my essay-poem from nine years earlier, where I imagined encoding a poem into protons and colliding it. We have since been brainstorming this poetry-physics experiment, writing poems and a scientific paper.

A visit to the library with archivist Anita Hollier during my first visit to CERN gave me the opportunity to see a copy of *The Copenhagen Faustparodie* (1932), a play about the discovery of the neutrino, one of the smallest and lightest elementary particles. The play was performed by students of Werner Heisenberg, Albert Einstein, and others at Niels Bohr's Institute for Theoretical Physics.[11] Neutrinos can pass through normal matter without detection and are candidates for a hypothesized form of dark matter. I had been interested in *Faustparodie* after learning about it in *Faust in Copenhagen* by Gino Segrè. I later read the play when I stumbled on it in the appendix of *Thirty Years That Shook Physics* (1966) by physicist George Gamow, who says that the authors and performers chose to be anonymous. Segrè, however, says that the play originated with Gamow and that physicist Max Delbrück was its primary author.[12] The play was later given quirky, handmade illustrations by Gamow and translated into English by him and his wife, Barbara Gamow. It is often regarded as an esoteric footnote of physics.

Faustparodie is based on Johann Wolfgang von Goethe's *Faust* (1808), where the character Faust makes a pact with the devil figure, Mephistopheles, to gain power and seduce his love interest, Gretchen. In *Faustparodie*, physicist Wolfgang Pauli, playing Mephistopheles, tries to convince physicist Paul Ehrenfest, playing Faust, of the existence of the neutrino, represented by Gretchen.[13] To demonstrate the uncertainty principle in quantum mechanics, where the non-commutation of position and momentum in subatomic particles is described in the equation $pq - qp = h/2\varpi i$, the character representing Charles Darwin turns himself into a Q for *position*, while the character representing physicist and astronomer Ralph Fowler turns himself into a P for *momentum*. They humorously leapfrog over one another. Below the scene, a stage direction says that at each exchange the sign $h/2\varpi i$, where i stands for the negative square root of one and h stands for Planck's constant, flashes.[14] As the sign flashes, a song is sung:

72 | THE IMAGINARY PRESENT

Thus exchanged are P and Q
  Time and time anew,
  Time and time anew.
Still there ever hovers by:
  h/2ϖi, h/2ϖi!

They can never rest in peace
  Till they're gone as geese,
  Till they're gone as geese.
Still there ever hovers by:
  h/2ϖi, h/2ϖi! [15]

Time and time anew.

During my first visit to CERN, I met theoretical physicist Luis Álvarez-Gaumé, who works on string theory, quantum field theory, cosmology, and particle physics at CERN and is also the director of Stony Brook University's Simons Center for Geometry and Physics, where I later served as the inaugural poet-in-residence. He and Juan José Gómez Cadenas met as young scientists at CERN and have been close friends since. Álvarez-Gaumé and I talked about physics, poetry, art, and the history of higher dimensions in geometry, starting with the Babylonians. The wall of his office featured a painting by the Surrealist artist, Salvador Dalí. On his blackboard, he taught me a new way to draw tesseracts, mathematical depictions of four or more spacetime dimensions. I had been using tesseracts for a poetry project after the poet Charles Stein had taught me how to draw them.

Álvarez-Gaumé's primary question as a theoretical physicist, he told me, is to explore whether the observer from classical behavior emerges from quantum behavior. When I asked if he has come to a conclusion, he said that he believes the answer depends on the observer. He said that we are so different from how we were when we were born that we are more like processes than beings. He said we must live with uncertainty and ignorance. Art is more fragile than science, he continued, because it cannot be repeated. Unlike scientists, he said, artists and poets create their own reality, including the rules of observation, meaning, and interpretation.[16]

He urged me to visit the Martin Bodmer Foundation, a book museum in Geneva that had scientific manuscripts by Nicolaus Copernicus, Johannes Kepler, and other scientists, as well as literary manuscripts by poets and writers, including Jorge Luis Borges. On my way there, I visited the grave of Borges, who had lived in Geneva as a child and then again later in life. As I was planning my outing, filmmaker and artist David Blair jokingly suggested in a text message to me from Paris that I give Borges a proton from the LHC.[17]

It was lightly raining at the graveyard, and the grounds were pocketed with small flower petals. I picked up a white petal, which resembled the white moth orchids I would soon see in the window in Paris three weeks later with David, momentarily confusing them with clouds in the sky. I found Borges's gravestone and placed the proton petal behind it. I thanked him for his labyrinths. In a playful story that I later wrote to David, I said that when I gave Borges the petal proton he had given me a positron, an antielectron particle that is a form of antimatter, the kind being studied in the Antimatter Factory at CERN. Since there is an asymmetry of matter and antimatter in the known universe, a problem in physics studied by Gómez Cadenas, I imagined that Borges, with his labyrinths, might know where the missing antimatter is located.

I learned about the asymmetry of matter and antimatter from a paper by Gómez Cadenas that he had sent me. I learned more in Canfranc, Spain, where I traveled after my first visit to CERN to attend the scientific review of a neutrino experiment called NEXT that Gómez Cadenas co-directs. I had been introduced to Gómez Cadenas by poet Rae Armantrout. Gómez Cadenas had helped translate some of her poems that reference physics for a Spanish edition of her poetry. The NEXT experiment, conducted at the Canfranc Underground Laboratory, a scientific research facility in an old train tunnel in the Spanish Pyrenees below a Baroque train station, is looking for a special kind of hypothesized neutrino, the Majorana fermion, that contains its own antimatter.[18] The train station and tunnel, I discovered, had been taken over by Nazis during World War II and transported Jewish prisoners to concentration camps. It also served as a site for those resisting the occupation. The tunnel reopened after the war and closed once again before the Spanish government dedicated it to scientific research many years later.

The universe is made mostly of matter, which contradicts evidence indicating that matter and antimatter are equally produced. If the Majo-

74 | THE IMAGINARY PRESENT

rana neutrino, the theorized subatomic particle and the only fermion that can contain its own antiparticle, does not exist, matter and antimatter would be perpetually competing in a universe that was explosive. Galaxies, planets, and people would not exist. The Majorana fermion is the most plausible mechanism to explain the asymmetry of matter and antimatter, Gómez Cadenas told me. The NEXT experiment is looking for it by searching for particles that display neutrinoless double beta decay, where two neutrons inside the nucleus of an atom are simultaneously transformed into two protons, or vice versa. The observation of neutrinoless double beta decay would determine that the neutrino being observed is a Majorana particle. Trying to observe neutrinoless double beta decay, Gómez Cadenas said, is like looking for a specific grain of sand on a large beach.[19]

In Canfranc, Gómez Cadenas told me about physicist Paul Dirac, who wrote an equation describing the motion of fermions, which differ from bosons like the Higgs. Dirac fermions don't contain their own antiparticles like the hypothesized Majorana fermion. If the Majorana fermion exists, its matter and antimatter would have the same mass but opposite electrical charges and quantum parts.[20] When I toured the Antimatter Factory at CERN, I took a picture of the first recorded image of antimatter. I used it as a graphic backdrop to a poem I wrote titled "Ace in the Hole" in which I write about quarks and James Joyce's *Finnegans Wake* (1939), which coined the word quark. Physicist Murray Gell-Mann first theorized the existence of quarks and named them after the word in *Finnegans Wake* since they come in threes. Physicist George Zweig also discovered quarks but called them "aces," the highest ranked playing cards in their suit. The poem explores the poetic dimensions of the number three by playing off of the dualism of inverted vowels in Buddhist koans, paradoxical statements or questions used in Buddhist teaching, and subatomic particles known as kaons. In the hotel kitchen at CERN I had met a physicist, Phil Rubin, who worked on kaons, and I immediately thought of koans.

The image of antimatter that I saw at the Antimatter Factory shows the size of antimatter in relation to 100 micrometers, ten thousandth of a meter. Making the image involves a photograph emitting light onto a radioactive isotope, Michael Doser explained, which then emits an electron. The image, which is the measurement of the antimatter itself, shows the shape of the spectral lines that are emitted in an antihydrogen atom. Seeing the image was like looking into the subspace of a visual poem. In Canfranc, as Gómez Cadenas and I discussed how antimatter was conceived of by theorists before it was discovered in experiments, he referenced the poem "The Unicorn," by poet Rainer Maria Rilke about the power of the imagination to invent:

> They fed him [the unicorn], not on ears of corn,
> but always on the possibility
> of being.[21]

Gómez Cadenas's cutting-edge search for the Majorana neutrino is driven by the possibility of its being, put forth by theoretical physicist Ettore Majorana, for which the Majorana fermion is named. Gómez Cadenas invited me to tour the underground neutrino experiment that is looking for the Majorana fermion. We traveled through the old train tunnels to the experiment by car. When we stepped out, we were in a long, underground passage at the opening of the NEXT experiment. Before we entered the experiment, Gómez Cadenas motioned toward me to join him in looking into one of the tunnels, where there was a light far away that led outside. *It's the light at the end of the tunnel!* he smiled. A few weeks later David joked with me, *Leave it to the scientist to show the poet the light at the end of the tunnel!*

Gómez Cadenas and I were photographed together with others in the tunnel. I also took three pictures of the tunnel, moving my hand each time to produce stuttering effects with the light at the end. In one of my photographs, there is a light trail that looks like musical notes. When the car I was riding in reached the end of the tunnel while leaving the facility after viewing the experiment, I thought of the positron, the antimatter that Borges had given me after I gave him the proton petal at his grave. As I passed the light at the end of the tunnel, I imagined the proton petal with the antimatter positron as a new kind of particle for a new kind of passage. "The Positron Passport," I called this new particle, is a document that contains its own antimatter like the theorized Majorana fermion. In quantum poetics, I operate this passport as a poetic device to travel deeper through the labyrinth that Borges used as a metaphor for the imagination.

Since the Majorana fermion is likely stable because it only weakly

76 | THE IMAGINARY PRESENT

interacts with its environment, scientists think it will be able to encode quantum information for quantum computing. In quantum theory, all particles, including the qubits being devised for quantum computers, exist in superposition, where they are in all possible states at the same time before coming into definite states after being observed or measured. Like poetry, physics complicates how existence is defined. In *Physics and Philosophy*, as Heisenberg explores the implications of quantum theory, he argues that for one to speak about subatomic particles, mathematics must be combined with a language that contains an ambiguous logic: "If one wishes to speak about the atomic particles themselves one must either use the mathematical scheme as the only supplement to natural language or one must combine it with a language that makes use of modified logic or of no well-defined logic at all."[22] Poetry makes use of both modified and no well-defined logic. It takes the imagination joined with rationality, informed by knowledge but not bound by certainty, to contend with the intrinsic ambiguities of both quantum theory and poetry in order to expand the possibilities spoken of by Rilke and his unicorn.

Technology acts as a human prosthetic, extending what can be experienced by the senses and conceived of by the mind. Poetry is an advanced technology like a particle collider or telescope, extending what can be experienced or thought. If there is no fixed, *a priori* reality, no axioms that exist outside of provisional circumstance and logical or creative convenience, both imagination and rationality lead to greater complexity rather than truth, dogma, and other absolutist concepts that arise from conventional adherences to universality.

In quantum poetics, spacetime and timespace as words reconceive the inseparability of space and time and the limitations of ordinary language to describe them. Heisenberg's attention to the role played by language in physics was encouraged by Niels Bohr.[23] Even in his comments on whether light is a wave or a particle, Heisenberg remarked that "the apparent duality arises in the limitations of our language."[24] Poetry has fewer limitations than ordinary language. Like light, poetry can be different things at once depending on how it is measured. At the beginning of "The Positron Passport," the shape on the page in manyworlds within superposition may be the wing of a bird that looks like a leaf. It may be a visual song that is a wing and a leaf. It may be a poem that is a birdsong shaped like a leaf on a page within the manyworlds of a book.

In Bashō's famous haiku, a frog leaps into a pond, and we hear the sound:

> The old pond—
> a frog jumps in,
> sound of water.[25]

The poem exhibits both quantum and classical behavior. Whereas the frog's leap into a pond is a quantum jump, since there is no reason given for the leap, cause and effect are at play in the transition from the second line, the action of the frog jumping, to the third line, the result of the jump. There's a quantum jump in the poem's form too. A spontaneous swerve occurs from the first line to the second line, from the description of the setting to the action of the jumping. The spacetime of the poem also communicates to the reader. We hear the sound of the water because the blank space upon which the letters are written is the old pond.

Language is not a virus from outer space as William S. Burroughs once dramatically proposed. Language is stranger than that, and so is outer space. Poetry is a hyperdimensional object of ordinary language in spacetime, unbound by the three dimensions of space and one dimension of time. Unlike a virus that replicates inside the cells of other organisms, poetry is a verb, an action like Bashō's jumping frog, that distorts the spacetime of language, acting upon it as a force like gravity acts upon matter.

In her poem "There is no Life or Death" (1914), poet Mina Loy evokes the radical revisions to common notions of spacetime that were a result of Einstein's theory of special relativity (1905), which explained how motion warps space and time because of the speed of light: "There is no Space or Time / Only intensity, / And tame things / Have no immensity."[26] While Loy doesn't address the principles of special relativity, she refutes the existence of space and time, challenging the common understandings to which these concepts were subjected, as Einstein did. If a poem is a hyperdimensional object of ordinary language distorting language like motion distorts spacetime in special relativity, it is not a tame thing. When poetry doesn't rely on received authority for its forms or ideas, as we see in the poetry of Loy and other literary nonconformists, and when scientists don't strictly rely on received authority for their experiments or

78 | THE IMAGINARY PRESENT

theories, as we see in Einstein's relativity, poetry and science speed past the ordinary parameters of reality, leaving "immensity" in their wake.

In my conversation with Gian Giudice at CERN, he said that physicists use axioms, statements claiming to be self-evidently true even though they are unproven. He said that they do so in order to think about physics problems without having to worry about, for example, what is happening on the moon. Poets like Loy not only use poetic logic to subvert axioms ("There is no Space or Time"), they create new axioms ("There is . . . / Only Intensity"), which results in new theoretical models for understanding reality.

A poem like Loy's can lift off like a rocket. A poem can memorialize the moon landing by describing the color of moon rocks. A poem can depict astronauts as they sleep while dreaming of the moon. A poem can make words weightless. A poem can be as mysterious as the moon. A poem can be as recognizable as the moon. A poem can be written on the American flag on the moon. The poem on the American flag on the moon can use the stripes as lines. A poem rejecting nationalism can be recited as all the flags on the moon are unplanted. Unplanting the flags on the moon can be a new action-poem. A new poem, just before it is written, is like a new moon. A poem can howl at the moon. In a poem, the moon can howl back. A poem can be the first poem to travel to the moon. A poem can fake a moon landing. A poem traveling to the moon can be written in moon dust. A poem can moon the moon. A poem can be "a moon in a dewdrop" (Dōgen).[27] A poem can be a moondew or a moondrop.

Sometimes poetry is the dewdrop's reflection that lets us see the moon inside of it. Sometimes poetry is the glass on a window that lets us see a dewdrop reflecting the moon. We look out windows assuming that what we see reveals what is beyond the glass, such as a moon, a dewdrop, or a moon inside a dewdrop. But sometimes we see reflections in a window that makes the window a mirror. The white moth orchids I saw in the window while visiting David in Paris after my visit to CERN first looked like clouds filling the sky. But there were no clouds that day. The only clouds were the ones in the window, reflecting the white moth orchids above and behind me. In that moment, the sky in my mind was filled with the manyworlds of birdsong sung in this poem, which is a window that when looked at is prose but when looked through is poetry.

A window is a threshold for sight. Sometimes we see what is inside

The Positron Passport | 79

and outside a window at the same time. Perhaps the third Shiva at CERN is looking out the window from inside a building next to the statue where the shadow Shiva dances. Perhaps the third Shiva is looking at the window from outside but only sees its own reflection, since windows, in certain light, are mirrors. Jorge Luis Borges used mirrors to symbolize multiple realities.

Quantum poetics incorporates what might be possible in a known universe mostly made of invisible dark energy and dark matter. According to Heisenberg, in quantum theory, the interaction between the observer and the object being observed causes "uncontrollable and large changes in the system being observed."[28] The concept of observation itself is indeterminate: "This indeterminateness of the picture of the process is a direct result of the indeterminateness of the concept 'observation'—it is not possible to decide, other than arbitrarily, what objects are to be considered as part of the observed system and what as part of the observer's apparatus."[29] A reader of a poem is an observer of the poem. The picture of the process of reading a poem is as indeterminate as an interpretation given to a poem by a reader.

But which is the observer and which the observable? The observer is never a static subject position in quantum theory. The observer influences what is being observed, just as the reader is never a static subject position in literature, since the reader influences the text being read. Since what is observed or read is based on the position in spacetime of the observer or reader, what is being observed or read cannot be considered to have an independent existence. The observer's agency to observe becomes an uncertain interaction between the observer and the observable. The reader's agency to read also becomes an uncertain interaction in the relationship between the reader and text. While modernism and postmodernism challenge certainty, do these systems of thinking go as far as quantum theory in directly rejecting the foundations of the certainty upon which classical mechanics and classical language depend?

The translation of quantum theory from mathematics to ordinary language is like any translation in that mistranslations occur because there are no one-to-one correspondences. For example, the "spin" of a subatomic particle is its angular momentum, which gives the particle a small, magnetic field. However, there is no classical analogue of the quantum property of spin, no translation of the property of spin to the

80 | THE IMAGINARY PRESENT

classical scale of matter. Particles with spin are not particles that rotate. In physics, where particles are imagined to be point-like rather than objects, the spin of a particle is an intrinsic property of the particle, often likened to mass. Imagining an angular momentum of a point-like particle that is not an object takes imagination, which is also needed to read the word *spin* but withhold conventional meanings while allowing for new definitions. Without one-to-one correspondences between classical logic and quantum logic, and without exact correspondences between ordinary language and literature, meaning in both science and literature is always variable.

Conventional authorities rarely treat the fields of poetry and physics together. In *Towards the Primeval Lightning Field* (1998) by poet Will Alexander, conventional authority is overturned by constructing one's "own thesis," as I attempt in quantum poetics:

> To conventional law I speak in linguistic cataract, my verbs with the tone of unstable altimeter. It is because I am between and between with my carking invisible gait, with my sustained suspension invisible to inwrought frailty of formula. Thus I can procure no clinical frame as holding myth, no pre-ingesting concept injected with synergy, no hoisted necromancer's pandect by which to describe the oasis across which I stutter. Because of this I am only eclectic oxygen symbols, by a mental war which magnetically inverses its riches. So I exist with a plenitude which symbol by symbol constructs its own thesis.[30]

Here, poetry is championed as a blurred vision and stutter resulting from opacities while speaking in a "linguistic cataract." The poet exists "between and between" with verbs that take on the tone of "unstable altimeter," radar used to determine altitude and the height of where one is in spacetime in relation to a horizon, where a line of sighted demarcation is no longer a viable sense to detect reliable information. It is the "plenitude" with which the poet exists that "constructs its own thesis," "symbol by symbol," into poetry and poetics.

The potential danger of any conventional authority is not to be underestimated. The atomic weapon was given authority by conventional law. Heisenberg was recruited to create the weapon for Germany during World War II, and it is not known if he intentionally sabotaged those efforts, or tried and failed. At CERN, Álvarez-Gaumé and I discussed new findings that suggested Heisenberg intended to make the weapon but made incorrect calculations. J. Robert Oppenheimer and Enrico Fermi were among the physicists at the Manhattan Project who made the weapon for the US and its allies. They recommended the weapon's use against Japan, serving on the Scientific Panel of the Interim Committee on Nuclear Power and advising the Target Committee on which cities to bomb.[31]

In contrast, physicist Bern Porter, who became a poet and advocated for the union of science and poetry in a literary practice he called Sciart, condemned the use of science for building the atomic weapon. As a physicist in his early thirties, Porter was drafted to contribute to the Manhattan Project, and, like many involved, didn't fully understand the project's mission because of its secrecy.[32] According to poet Mark Melnicove, who knew Porter and became his literary executor, the atomic weapons dropped on Japan emotionally traumatized Porter because of his participation in their creation.[33] When the war was over and Porter's position was to be terminated, he quit, though later he was involved with the Saturn V moon rocket project and advocated for nuclear power plants and the so-called Atoms for Peace program.[34] Still, he remained grief-stricken throughout his life by his participation in the Manhattan Project. In the introduction of Melnicove's edited volume of Porter's writing, Sounds That Arouse Me (1993), he explains that the use of the atomic weapon created a split within Porter between the scientist and the artist. It was because of this split that Porter, with Sciart, aimed to integrate art's transcendent properties with science's potential for harmony with nature.[35]

When talking with scientists, I sometimes introduce the term poethics, which originates from Joan Retallack's book The Poethical Wager and describes an approach to making art modeled on how we aspire to live. Science happens within larger cultural domains, and while there are scientists who work to keep science from being used for destructive purposes, the development of the atomic weapon and other weaponry since demonstrates that the scientific community does not sufficiently practice poethics by making science modeled on ethical behavior. "War is a mental disorder of the highest order," according to Porter in his poem "Growing Up in the Nuclear Age" (1978), which narrates how, while working for the Manhattan Project, he learned that the atomic weapon had been dropped on Hiro-

82 | THE IMAGINARY PRESENT

shima.[36] Porter's *Sciart* is a form of poethics by engaging poetry and science through ethics. Poethics can be used to help guide scientists toward ethical uses of their work as they pursue scientific knowledge.

Like poets, scientists also need ambitious imaginations. Scientists Niayesh Afshordi, Robert B. Mann, and Razieh Pourhasan once published a paper theorizing that our three-dimensional universe was created by the formation of a black hole from an exploding star in a four-dimensional universe. Our universe, they suggested, is a hologram of the collapsing star, existing behind the three-dimensional event horizon.[37] If our universe is a photograph of

an illuminated
interference pattern,
a hologram producing
a three-dimensional image
created from a four-dimensional
black hole
of an exploding star,
what dimension
is the photograph
of the white moth orchids
taken in Paris, the clouds
upon which
these letters
fly,
their wings
opening and closing
and opening
like the spine of
The Positron Passport
in the window
of this poem
that reflects the
indeterminate
sky?

To Be in Any Form

"To be in any form, what is that?" (Walt Whitman).[1] Quantum poetics does not stop at semiotics or procedure. *To be in any form, what is that?* By applying principles in physics to poetry, and principles in poetry to physics, quantum poetics investigates how physical reality is assumed, imagined, and tested through language at both discernible and indiscernible scales of spacetime. *To be in any form, what is that?* Theoretical physics illustrates that uncertainty is a condition of material reality. *To be in any form, what is that?* A poem in any form might be a shifting-eye picture keeping watch on an ideology. *To be in any form, what is that?* A poem might be a slapstick criticism of the superserious or an unfathomable song. *To be in any form, what is that?* A poem might be a visual translation of canonical poems created from an algorithm that produces outspread, humming-creatures (see Eric Zboya). *To be in any form, what is that?* "... Let up again to feel the puzzle of puzzles ..." (Whitman again).[2]

The Password to the Quantum Supercomputer Poem Will Be NCC-1701

My poetic forms are all rocket ship these days. In superstring theory, time is a cubist face of space. Like a hand on the anywhere, in slight repose. Or, more threadbare: "Beware of all enterprises that require new clothes" (oh, Thoreau!).[1]

Progress, scientific or artistic, might best be considered in the context of novelty rather than evolution, where a *pre* and a *post* accelerate through Alfred Jarry's *Imaginary Present*. The *pre* of quantum poetics includes *pre*-science, but also *prescience*.

That is not to say that quantum poetics is not all scientific method, too, wanting to invent new tech for the poem, for you. Let's consider *Star Trek*. Enterprise engineer Scotty, upon discovering how his future-self develops the Federation's first Trans-Warp technology, which permits the transportation of people on and off starships traveling at warp speed, remarks, As One Might In a Poem, "It never occurred to me to think of space as the thing that was moving."[2] This sentence is a good example of the glitter.

Shall I become "a transparent eye-ball?" (Ralph Waldo Emerson).[3] Emerson again, just past the occasion of glittering, where form makes spacetime: "Words are the finite organs of the infinite mind."[4]

The Violet Doorway

Samsara Congeries (2016), mIEKAL aND's ambidextrous epic of deep time and polyvalent dimension, is written in a "splitting language" where linguistic, visual, and alphabetic architecture meet at a startling, interactive complexity.[1] Throughout this 500-page, forty-year-long serial poem, a propulsive "actual imaginary" undermines entrenched conceptions of reality, self, language, and literary form, offering instead an emergent and approximate spacetime, at once subterranean and extraterrestrial, nowhere and everywhere.

The poem is written in fourteen books sculpted by the occult speech acts of different narrators, conceivably the iterations of a reincarnated self in the Samsara cycle of birth and death to which the title refers. The typescripts introducing each book and internal fonts vividly shift, reading like personalities or characters. The scope of forms and characters, and the focus on language as a material construct mediated through fluid acts of perception and desire, position the text as a transhuman travelogue, one of a traveler outside of spacetime or a collective identity inside all times. In this context, the poem is a ship of spacetime.

The artistic lineage of this work includes many who, like the author, live and make experimental art outside the mainstream. *Samsara Congeries* is an extraordinary contribution to the experimental, an extension of the experimental life of mIEKAL aND, known for his leadership in global DIY and anarchist art networks, his pioneering work in electronic literature and typography, his collaborative books of poetry, his innovative publishing initiatives, and his hypermedia organic-farming community and home at Dreamtime Village in Wisconsin. *Samsara Congeries* cannot be read without engaging in a novel experience with language, where the open and critical mind moves with the poem into previously inaccessible realms, waking up to lucidly dream in its textual village. This book, like

86 | THE IMAGINARY PRESENT

the author's life, itself a poem, is an artistic and political intervention of the poetic mind within our dire time.

mIEKAL aND's name, written in tOGGLE cASE, is a conceptual subterfuge, unlike *Samsara Congeries*, the book, which is more a vast interweaving of Dada & soundpo & vispo & activist elegy & the uncensored mind & archaic-futuristic possibility. It is a reincarnating anarchist's confessional poem. It is a sustained inquiry into language & visual form & reality & it's so *post-post* it's *pre*. It goes deep to the private inside-someone. Each book in the book becomes more abstract, more "panshaman," more "shacknasty jack," unlike the entities at the beginning such as the "healing guest" or the unnatural "trance songs," which assert recognizable orders of reality.[2] Later, something is sung "as a wet line knots easily."[3] He & she & children are quipu knots & letter-poems & play-poems.[4] There is an imaginary number from which *Samsara Congeries* is created in the chapter of meta, where a person is born.[5]

The poet in the book is a visual bookmaker. The book's hypersphere is alive with an Energy Church & an Elder So & a Sha Long & a Traggy Fineleaf & a merchant & Wm Blake & One Dickinson & The Small Press & Men Tell Slow Stories & ART ROTATES THE EMPIRE & the alphabet of non-iconography. We see Svengali & Joseph Beuys & Gertrude Stein & Kenneth Patchen & Gurdjieff & The College of Immortals & Duchamp & Apollinaire & a "Faceted surface face and tentative Duchamp" & a symbol-tinged bachelor & an SASE John & a Mary Addams & the internal verbio wanderer, a whole species of references suggestive of a "polyTransArt" criticism.[6] The poem is a tech manual for the imagination. The fiction has been installed.

In book nine of Samsara Congeries, titled "L=I=N=G=L=A=G=E," an homage to the L=A=N=G=U=A=G=E school of poetry and its seminal journal edited by poets Bruce Andrews and Charles Bernstein, mIEKAL disrupts our assumptions about first-person point of view and the ordinary limits of language. Like some of the theorists and practitioners of L=A=N=G=U=A=G=E poetry, mIEKAL combines personal observation and experience with disturbed syntax and grammar, bringing into question the assumed agency of the speaker.

In "L=I=N=G=L=A=G=E," the "A" is replaced by an "I," and the "U" is replaced by an "L." This is funny, and critically significant, because L=A=N=G=U=A=G=E poetry challenges normative conceptions of self-

The Violet Doorway | 87

hood, and poetic content as a whole, that argues for transcendence and universality, all problematic extensions of capitalism and patriarchy to writers of L=A=N=G=U=A=G=E poetry. L=I=N=G=L=A=G=E poetry extends L=A=N=G=U=A=G=E poetry by replacing the "A" with the "I," letting the poem do the talking. Replacing the "A" with the "I" re-imagines the "I" by redefining the material body of L=A=N=G=U=A=G=E poetry itself, which are the letters, of course, the "L" through the "E." Similarly, the "U" (which can be read as the reader, the companion to the "I") is replaced by an "L." What does this "L" stand for? Language! This hyperbolic poetic gesture of L=I=N=G=L=A=G=E engages L=A=N=G=U=A=G=E poetry by asserting a textural self, one encoded by poetic practice into L=A=N=G=U=A=G=E poetry's critique of agency as a linguistic construct, a critique they made that was inspired, in part, by poststructuralism and Marxism. The "I" of L=I=N=G=L=A=G=E, as in L=A=N=G=U=A=G=E poetry, is not the capitalist "I" of exploitative history but the transhuman, liberated "I/eye" of Samsara that changes as it reincarnates through the life and death cycle of the poem, ever mutable, beyond stasis, reaching outside the stronghold of consensus reality. L=I=N=G=L=A=G=E is an occult extension of L=A=N=G=U=A=G=E poetry's critiques of language, myth, and capitalism.

My response to mIEKAL's poem just got much more "deloraloriolius," as "Lettrist fixates taper an irregular-only mark."[7] In other words: "i ist nomeromerorder ismist!"[8]

In *Samsara Congeries*, meaning is emergent and contextual, not absolute. In the book, I (the Samsara "I," which is also the reader) am a world that never ends because I begin in a future that is constructed in the present. When language takes on the fluidity of poetic thinking, it cannot be easily controlled or purified. Poetry, like all art forms subsumed by the constraints of ongoing empire, is a method of resisting empire from the inside out when it seeks liberation.

Samsara Congeries achieves liberation through its resistance. It is a "solar emissary" sent on a special mission under the spell of Dada artist and poet Kurt Schwitters.[9] There is an "immaculate submission" of "carat lines" & a single sentence in a single setting & the luscious "Bystandardesque." André Breton is there as is the hilarious "Libido dildo" with all of its phallic l's and i's & facing b's and d's.[10] There's the abracadabra of a Mayan ruin & "The Missing Text of the Lost Tower" & negative-numbered foot-

THE IMAGINARY PRESENT

notes. A "4-D space crunch" happens alongside email poems. Its neologisms will enhance your dream vocabulary.

Someday, when you are visiting Dreamtime Village, when the fog will soon unroll across the hills during your morning departure, be sure to ask mIEKAL who Cybele-mon is & learn that she is a fortune teller from his past. Then talk in her "linguaMOO." Let your elementary particles spin in Cybele's "multiverse garden," because you are already there.[11] Upon leaving, he reads "The Sorrow Project: 1000 notes lining the habitat" from *Samsara Congeries* to me:

> *amorous season forced to part*
> *dreams can't reach a perfect time*
> *seize the wind, see nothing*[12]

A Morse-code-like gate of dashes, equal signs, and vertical lines follows this passage in the book as it does elsewhere. The last poem addresses the "beginning of the era of dissolution."[13] *Samsara Congeries* ends aND continues to travel, all ways.

Poetry in Superposition

Poetry, like the mathematical formalisms of quantum systems that capture what can be potentially actualized through observation, moves outside of the scope of normative language, which assumes that it constitutes the "actual": today, for instance, is both strata and subspace. Which spiral arm? Your arrow of time is all or nothing. Yet the unnamed sky keeps arriving without limit. Stop us if you can.

Poetry can be treated as a dynamic complex system that increases in complexity as its interactive elements increase, though not toward fundamental synthesis, narrative, and ethics or spatial, temporal, and conceptual direction. As each element becomes more interactive, a poem becomes less chiral, more multiversal, more *immarginable* (Joyce).[1] Even at rest, our wings spread against a hazy horizon, we fly.

Poetry is not a lighthouse that guides ships through disorienting water; poetry is the water, which can be dangerous, as Plato knew. When water is not dangerous, it is density and delirium. When poetry is not water, it is the indeterminate line where water and ocean floor meet. Sometimes poetry is the bathysphere that travels here. Matter compresses in the gravity underwater. Without gravity, a poem breaks apart.

Poetry is a galaxy mediating strong and weak gravity. Outside each galaxy, gravity is altered by a dark energy that transforms gravity into a repulsive force that moves matter from matter, which makes spacetime expand between galaxy clusters, growing the universe faster and faster. Like a poem, the universe is a complex system that becomes more complex in spacetime as its interactive elements increase.

Poetry at the boundary of gravity is a galaxy that compresses and expands. Since the spacetime between galaxy clusters is expanding at an accelerating rate because of dark energy, which alters how gravity behaves at cosmological scales outside of galactic systems, the boundary

| 89

90 | THE IMAGINARY PRESENT

near a galaxy where gravity compresses and expands deviates, too, binding matter inside the galaxy while unbinding matter beyond it.

Poetry is not only *the nature of things* (Lucretius) but the things of nature, including nature at quantum and cosmological scales, where wilderness is simultaneously its elemental parts and the effects it produces outside of local ecologies.[2] Poetry and quantum gravity are entanglements of quantum and relativistic states. Like the spin of a subatomic particle, entanglement is an intrinsic property of matter.

Poetry in quantum superposition is without direction, moving by quantum jump, subverting the law of deterministic causality. Poetry in superposition is not entropic, declining into disorder, but endemic to its everywhere and everywhen. A state beyond the "actual," quantum superposition defeats the dogma of the ideal, the power of the primordial. Constelled in superposition, we radiate, we burst.

Poetry as light is both a wave and a particle, energy and matter, before its wavefunction collapses when written and read. While the literary artform of poetry may appear to be capable of shape-shifting in any direction within spacetime, it is each direction and spacetime that shapeshift. Some choreographies in a poem seem clear: The rocket lifts off. But once past the heliopause, *we laugh into our green beards* (Jarry).[3]

Poetry is not only entangled with the inner and outer limits of its elemental parts, where it is capable of communicating with other quantum states instantaneously across distances, it is also entangled with the conditions of its own inception and cessation. Poiesis in spacetime is an activity where beginning and ending meet and release, release and meet, a river we travel that flows each way at once.

Poetry is as incomplete as an x-ray, as polished as a prism. Like the geography of grooves and ridges in a human neocortex, the folds of a poem increase its surface area. Oscillating at all scales by extending and collapsing spacetimes between them, a poem is an expanding universe that is a poem that is a portal, quickening travel among the distances it grows. Transdimensional, hydroelectric, our currents carry.

$U+F+O+L+A+N+G+U+A+G+E$

Poet, scholar, and artist Christine Wertheim, in her book *mUtter—bAbel* (2014), tells the "story of a language" through hand-drawn and typographical visual poems that sonically treat words as "vOcal Organs" by highlight the letter o[1]. Investigating the concept of motherhood and a "mOther tOngue" through a kinetic range of material renderings of the letter o, the book can be read alongside superstring theory, which has proposed that all matter is made from open and closed subatomic membranes of energy that vibrate.

The letter o, topologically similar to a closed string in superstring theory, is in constant motion in the book, often abstracted through subjects such as openings, orgasms, and nothings. The political dimensions of *mUtter—bAbel* address, among other crises, the human movement across the US-Mexican border through intellectual and emotional outrage for the racially bigoted and dehumanizing conditions endured by migrants. Here, I'm reminded of the way that proposed dimensions in superstring theory are bordered by "branes," the points upon which open and closed strings are situated. Even in physics a border is a body politic.

Visual poetry, because of its direct interaction with the spacetime of the page, is especially capable of exploring the concept of dimensionality. "Flatland: A Romance of Many Dimensions" (2013) by poet Derek Beaulieu enacts the variability of spacetime by using Edwin Abbott Abbott's 1884 novel, for which the poem is named, where characters are geometric shapes in a two-dimensional world.[2] Beaulieu challenges the conventions of reading and writing by replacing the subject matter of Abbott's novel with his graphical representations:

> I began by photocopying each page. . . . I then identified each unique
> letter on the first line of each page, and traced a line—using a light-

| 91

92 | THE IMAGINARY PRESENT

table, ink and a rule—from the first occurrence of each letter on the first line through the first appearance of each of those same letters on each subsequent line. . . . By reducing reading and language into paragrammatical statistical analysis, content is subsumed into graphical representation of how language covers a page.[3]

If one imagines a page as a two-dimensional representation of the universe and a poem on a page as a three-dimensional representation of the multiverse, the theorized collection of many universes, Beaulieu's "Flatland: A Romance of Many Dimensions" can be seen as a geo(graphical) representation of hyperdimensional spacetime. It demonstrates how literature can exist in many spacetimes at once, from the two- to four-dimensional world of Abbott's novel to the theoretically and physically expanded dimensions of Beaulieu's visual and statistical translation, which creates a post-fourth dimension forged by poetic procedure.

The fourth dimension is where the three dimensions of space join with the dimension of time, but in superstring theory, at least ten dimensions of spacetime are thought to be possible. While higher dimensions have been a subject of art and literature before, Beaulieu's poem suggests that we are not in a post- or double-post literary postmodernism but something else entirely, where chronological markers such as "post" and "pre" have no meaning. In the hypothesized multiverse of multiple dimensions of spacetime, the notion of historical linearity, which relies on the outdated idea that time moves like an arrow through a past, present, and future, is as one dimensional as one of the drawn lines in Beaulieu's multidimensional poem.

While we might ordinarily assume that the multiple dimensions theorized in superstring theory exist at scales larger than the known universe, they are often theorized at the subatomic scale, smaller than the smallest known elementary particles. Poet Jennifer K. Dick, in her book *CERN 200*, explores this scale, what she calls the "subsubatomic," and how the search for these new physics is like the search that poets take on for new forms of language:

I dreamt the firewall debate only engendered slews of new language until the O.E.D. could no longer keep up with the scientific lingo being born daily, hourly, by the minute and second. Subsubatomic particles beyond Leptons, neutrinos, the Higgs Bosons, Cherenkov detectors and particulates of spooky matter meant to be quantum post-post pre-octanic subor or postorganic space rooting in the rayites of bits of bundles of blotchers needing names for whatever that green goo was or could be a line crossing an advanced version of a nuclear electroinstascope— but then even those words were brought into doubts by SoupCanning Maldacena theories of particulate redirections. Translators, linguists and theorists alike were collapsing from exhaustion, servers and backup generators were being fried, bundles of wires in and out of cerebral cortexes were called into question until there was nothing left to do but unplug it all, go dark, pause, wait, sleep.[4]

These poems by Wertheim, Beaulieu, and Dick are all examples of what I call "U+F+O+L+A+N+G+U+A+G+E." As unidentified flying objects of language, the poems are meant to be visually and semantically unfamiliar. They use new forms of language and image to travel as spacetimeships. We also see this travel in the textile poems of poet-critic Maria Damon, where she weaves visual poems by opening and closing strings of yarn. In her visual textile poem "Poetics as a Theory of Everything" (2014), a reference to the Theory of Everything in physics that attempts to reconcile relativity with quantum theory, and which she made as the cover image for a book of the same name by poet Ira Livingston, what everything means is the question.

The Subtle Web of Thought

In an interview later in his life with the American Institute of Physics, Werner Heisenberg discusses how Niels Bohr, his mentor before the two became divided over the race for the atomic weapon during World War II, was more concerned if a theory in physics was conceptually accurate than if it conformed to data or mathematics.[1] Bohr's influence on Heisenberg's commitment to conceptual and mathematical accuracy likely strengthened his ability to investigate the theoretical dimensions of quantum theory in relation to language. In *Physics and Philosophy*, he references Johann Wolfgang von Goethe's *Faust* after discussing the problem that quantum theory does not have a language beyond mathematics to describe it.[2] He quotes Mephistopheles, who says that while formal education instructs that logic braces the mind "in Spanish boots so tightly laced" and that even spontaneous acts require a sequential process:

> In truth the subtle web of thought
> Is like the weaver's fabric wrought:
> One treadle moves a thousand lines,
> Swift dart the shuttles to and fro,
> Unseen the threads together flow,
> A thousand knots one stroke combines.[3]

Mephistopheles is arguing that creative thinking goes far beyond sequential logic. The "subtle web of thought" that occurs in the mind happens when one lever or poetic maneuver moves many ideas at once, which makes the ideas flow together quickly in unseen ways. While on the surface representing the devil, and thus a malignant, supernatural figure to whom Faust must sell his soul to gain what he desires, Mephistopheles also symbolizes logic, knowledge, and authority. He acts as a sophisti-

The Subtle Web of Thought | 95

cated advocate of materialism and skepticism, concepts deeply embedded within the scientific worldview.

Heisenberg says that the passage from which the quote by Mephistopheles appears "contains an admirable description of the structure of language and of the narrowness of the simple logical patterns."[4] His comment speaks to his interest in broadening what constitutes logic and the inability of ordinary language to describe what happens inside of an atom. Quantum poetics extends this idea by exploring how poetic thinking can describe the quantum world.

Poetry, as a complex form of creativity using language, functions as a literary shorthand like "one treadle" moving "a thousand lines," where a "thousand knots one stroke combines." One stroke of the treadle, the lever on a loom that weaves the fabric of thought referenced in *Faust*, generates "a thousand knots" or sites of complexity in a poem. Poetic thinking condenses language into these sites of complexity using the imagination, which is mechanized into a material reality through literary devices, creating textiles that we call poems.[5]

Shorthand, which lessens the amount of spacetime it takes for information to travel, evokes the concept of an Einstein-Rosen Bridge, a spatiotemporal wormhole, which connects sites in different spacetimes together, creating passage. Is a poem a wormhole made of language?

Physicists today consider how the open and closed strings of superstring theory might function as elementary constituents of matter. Like poets, physicists think through multiple forms of language, and in quantum poetics, where creative reading attentive to physics is conducted, the open and closed strings of superstring theory can be interpreted in relation to the open and closed texts proposed by Lyn Hejinian in her essay "The Rejection of Closure" (1983).[6]

In superstring theory, a closed string is topologically equivalent to a circle, having no end points, whereas an open string is topologically equivalent to a line interval, having two end points. According to Hejinian, one possible characterization of a closed text is "one in which all the elements of the work are directed toward a single reading of it" and "each element confirms that reading and delivers the text from any lurking ambiguity."[7] A closed text, then, might be visualized as a circle, as having no beginning and no end points in which the reader imaginatively "enters" or "exits" the text. This situates the writing and reading of a

96 | THE IMAGINARY PRESENT

closed text within the circle's interior, where, Hejinian says, "all the elements of the work are directed."

Hejinian argues that an open text within experimental writing traditions, such as those in L=A=N=G=U=A=G=E poetry, of which she was a part, "foregrounds process," "invites participation," and is "open to the world and particularly to the reader."[8] Open texts have end points, entries and exits in which the reader participates. An open text operates outside of a closed text's interior circle, its extended topology uncurling into a line, one that is both topological and poetic. Hejinian, using the subtle web of thought, casts the line farther, saying, "Writing's forms are not merely shapes but forces."[9]

Metaphor and Decay

In physics, decay means "transformation." Since matter cannot be destroyed but can only be redistributed as energy or another form of matter, annihilation is an antecedent to novelty, produced by change. In poetry, distinct objects compared in metaphor are changed, or made novel, by the act of comparison, suggestive of how matter is changed by observation in quantum theory. A subatomic particle in quantum superposition exists in all points of space at the same time within a state of potentiality or possibility. Werner Heisenberg, in *Physics and Philosophy*, says that "the transition from the 'possible' to the 'actual' takes place during the act of observation."[1] In quantum physics, observation is the material mechanism that produces the transformation of the possible to the actual. Poets, too, have seen such decay as transformation: "And now [the grass] seems to me the beautiful uncut hair of graves" (Walt Whitman).[2]

The Origami Time Machine

In Grant Morrison's comic book series *The Invisibles*, released monthly from 1994 to 2000, the character Ragged Robin uses a timesuit built from a time machine that looks like paper folded as origami. The timesuit comes from both the past and the future of the comic's present time, which is 1997. She uses it to travel from her future in 2012, the year the Mayan calendar ended, into the past, which is her present, where she experiences time as a hologram of two universes overlapping. She says of the hologram: "I could see all of it and . . . it wasn't exactly **below** me, it was something **else**; I'd moved in a direction I hadn't even **thought** of until then."[1] Poems, too, can move us in directions we had not thought of until reading or writing the poem. The key to Ragged Robin's timeline integrity is a photograph that she carries of two cloud patterns exactly the same, taken in different places at different times: "Fractal patterns **repeat** themselves through time, like backgrounds in **cartoons**."[2] It is no surprise that the photograph represents objective reality, the key to time travel for Ragged Robin as she works to bring back items from the future back to the present that will trigger a Time-Scientist to build the origami time machine that she uses. When the Time-Scientist is looking at her photograph, he is more interested in the material that is used for the photograph than the cloud patterns depicted, suggesting that the material medium of the photograph is just as significant to the origami time machine as the images it contains. The origami time machine is about space and time and the machine they make. It is about the folds in spacetime that a poem can make.

The Physics of Existence

Rae Armantrout has over seventy poems that reference physics, starting with "Engines," her 1983 and 1992 collaboration with poet Ron Silliman. Both poets are associated with L=A=N=G=U=A=G=E poetry. In their poem, they refer to a massless subatomic particle that is not a neutrino and yet is created in what is known in physics as beta decay, in which a subatomic beta particle is emitted from an atomic nucleus, decaying or transforming the original particle. "The semblance of existence lurks in the verb," they write, exploring particle physics alongside grammar. They are also thinking about what is meant by the appearance of existence versus existence itself, a concern that emerges often in Armantrout's work.[1]

Armantrout's poems work at the edges of the unknown. Her poetic vision is peripheral and fractured, speaking to the uncertainties and indeterminacies in quantum physics. The foregrounding of the materiality of language in her poetry aligns it with the investigations of the material universe that happen in physics.

Her poem "Chirality" (2015) begins: "If I didn't need / to do anything, / would I? // Would I oscillate in two or three dimensions?"[2] The narrator is speaking both as a human and a particle of matter that is oscillating as one would in superstring theory. By making one persona of the poem a subatomic particle, she investigates her subject in a way that only a poem can, by being the subject. A few stanzas later, she writes, "A massless particle / passes through the void / with no resistance."[3] Here, she is referencing a massless particle such as a neutrino, which is almost weightless and passes through most forms of matter. Exploring what a neutrino is in the context of space and time, she says, "Ask what it means / to pass through the void. // Ask how it differs / from not passing."[4] By writing a poem about this question, she is asking similar questions that physicists ask except with the advantage of poetic form.

100 | THE IMAGINARY PRESENT

"Chirality," the poem's title, refers to an object that cannot be superimposed on its mirror image, such as human hands, but it also evokes matter-antimatter asymmetry. Physicists are interested in the asymmetry of matter and antimatter in the universe, since there is more matter than antimatter. Theorized subatomic particles such as neutrinos like the Majorana fermion are thought to contain their own antiparticles and being studied to learn more about the asymmetry of matter and antimatter. A particle that contains its own antimatter exhibits chirality, where its matter cannot be superimposed on its mirror antimatter.

The first two stanzas of Armantrout's poem "Dress Up" (2013) explore what existence means by rearranging material in *The Little Book of String Theory* (2010) by physicist Steven Gubser. The poem references a "dressed" electron that emits virtual particles, which spontaneously jump in and out of existence. The particles are real and not real depending on how reality is defined. The poem ends with the image of a toddler waiting for the speaker and her companions to "get the joke // about being here, being there."[5] The image of the toddler dressing up plays off of the "dressed" electron that emits virtual particles. The phrase "being here, being there" evokes wave-particle duality in physics, where light can be a wave or a particle depending on how it is observed. It also evokes Gertrude Stein's phrase "There is no there there," the elsewhere and everywhere that is not somewhere or nowhere. In "Dress Up," the electron and the toddler both "exist" in costume, which is consensus reality, the reality that people agree is real but which, in quantum physics, is not independently real. The adults viewing the toddler also exist in the costume of reality, but unlike the toddler, they are unaware of it.

In other poems by Armantrout, we see phenomena in physics satirically collaged with everyday objects. In "Accounts" (2013), she interrupts her commentary on the speed of light with a drinking cup that has the slogan, "Thinking of you!"[6] An ordinary cup with a superficial social nicety disrupts a known constant in the universe. This collaging of a law of physics with an everyday object displaying a slogan is a signature gesture in Armantrout's poetry, and we see a similar move in her poem "Material" (2015), which juxtaposes physics with consumerism.

"Material" opens with dry, infomercial speak: "Oh, you're wearing the gold one. // That's my favorite / to be honest. // The gun metal is all gone."[7] The preferred gunmetal color of the clothing in the infomercial

The Physics of Existence | 101

is sold out, and the gold color is being sold instead. The poem moves into a discussion about how we exist as infinitesimal points, a theory by physicist Brian Cox. The poem says that the infinitesimal points contain "empty pockets," and in the last sentence, we are back to the infomercial clothing: "Here, you try it on."[8] The "empty pockets" of the infinitesimal points of which we may be made also exist as pockets on the infomercial clothing, which we try on, dressing up again in the clothing of reality like we see in the poem "Dressed Up."

But what does it mean that we "consist of" the empty pockets of infinitesimal points in the universe as well as the empty pockets of clothing in the infomercial? Both are empty, without material substance or artistic depth. Plus, the physical reality where the infinitesimal points exist is similar to the virtual reality where the infomercial exists. Here, existence is explored through both physical and virtual environments. The poem prompts us to ask, in relation to its title: How can we seem so full of "material"—the materiality of existence, the materiality of the body, and the materiality of subatomic particles—while being empty, too?

Emptiness can be material because what we mean by empty and material is more complex than these terms initially signal. In both poetry and physics, existence is more nuanced than ordinary language can describe. Armantrout's poem reveals the contradiction of materiality as emptiness and, in doing so, illustrates the limitations of ordinary language to describe the extraordinary aspects of reality that poetry and quantum theory expose. Materiality can be empty in the way that a neutrino is a weightless subatomic particle without mass, so it makes sense, as she says in "Material," for us "to consist / of infinitesimal points."[9] She introduces the empty pockets in the clothing on the virtual infomercial alongside the empty pockets in the infinitesimal points, which is another way we can be empty and material at the same time, a so-called contradiction that requires no resolution. The emptiness in the infinitesimal points is similar to the emptiness in the clothing's pockets and the infomercial's virtual speech. The poem illustrates that which is not easily seen otherwise. Complex instruments of measurement like the theory of infinitesimal points, and the poem itself, are needed to detect the emptiness of material reality. What we mean by measuring or observing reality depends entirely upon our terms, both Armantrout's poem and quantum theory asserts, and as our language is renovated to respond to discoveries

102 | THE IMAGINARY PRESENT

in quantum physics, so must our conceptions of existence and reality.

In her poem "Around" (2009), Armantrout contends with her mortality in relation to time and what she calls its pendulous loops, which have meaning, "*this* meaning," she writes, pointing to the poem itself, where the italicized *this* exists.[10] The poem presents a scene where she and her husband have found a spot where her ashes will be scattered upon her death. They are being shown this spot, she writes, "by a sort of realtor," highlighting how shopping for a place of final rest in death is like shopping for a house.[11] The scene is narrated with an emotional detachment but tethered by the earlier passage about time and its pendulous loops. It's followed by a statement about time in quotations, indicating another slogan: "The future / is all around us." Outside of the quotation marks she writes, "It's a place," talking about the future, and then, in a new stanza, "anyplace / where we don't exist."[12] The future is any place where we don't exist. She makes time a physical space, not a period of duration that can happen without us, which speaks to the physical place where her ashes can be scattered. The stanza break in between "It's a place" and "anyplace / where we don't exist" is a structural break in space and time, and not just in the spacetime of the poem. The break is just long and short enough in space and time for the reader to experience their own mortality, their own absence, in this blank part of the poem's page, the empty spacetime between stanzas. Here, the space and time in the poem are interacting with the reader's experience of space and time, unifying them.

In "Passage" (2009), Armantrout writes, "I existed finally / as the idea / of temporal extension" with the idea that the speaker exists as time extended into the three dimensions of space.[13] Existence, in this context, is what she calls later in the poem a "Double-meaning," a quantum "superposition," where subatomic particles exist in all possible points in space at the same time. These lines are followed by the image of a creature appearing larger and more ferocious than it is.[14] The image brings poetic nuance to the concept of superposition, asking what is real and what is not, what appears to be real, and what appears to be something it is not, nuances that also happen between the possible and the actual in quantum physics.

Armantrout's poem "Spin" (2011) references the quantum mechanical property of spin in subatomic particles. Despite the word for "spin," subatomic particles do not rotate but possess spin, which is an intrinsic property of particles much like mass. Physicists describe spin as an angular momentum of a subatomic particle. Armantrout's poem "Spin" talks about particles having spin but no dimension or volume and depth, and yet these particles are said to exist. The poem asks: How is this possible? However, this question is not asked directly as it would be in prose. Instead, as a poem, the question is asked through offering information about the particles and then moving on to two sections, one describing the speech of a political candidate and the other, the statement "Light strikes our eyes / and we say, Look *there!*"[15]

This moment is like her earlier examination of "being here, being there" in "Dress Up." Whereas the dressed electron emitting virtual particles points to being here and being there at the same time, in "Spin," to get to "*there,*" we have to speak and say, "Look," after the light has struck our eyes. In the poem, seeing "there" is a mechanical process mediated by light, the eyes, and, most importantly, poetic gesture. It is the poem that directs the reader to encounter what they ordinarily take for granted: seeing. In the context of physics and everyday experience, we might encounter the idea of existence, the generic language of a politician, or light striking the eyes, but in the poem, we encounter these conditions as linked settings on the page. It is *there,* in the spacetime of the page itself, where we begin to "see" that the politician's empty phrasing is the dimensionless point that theoretically spins the way news spins: it has no depth.

Werner Heisenberg, in *Physics and Philosophy,* says that we do not directly see nature: "We have to remember that what we observe is not nature in itself but nature exposed to our method of questioning."[16] A poem is a novel method of questioning. We can only see "there" when the light in the poem allows us to see "there." This is where a quantum poetical reading of Armantrout's poetry is necessary, just as a quantum poetical reading of quantum theory is necessary. The poem is itself an occasion where observation is directed, except it doesn't point us to a static reality narrowed by a realist perspective that is presumed to be happening only here or only there. Instead, Armantrout's poetry suggests that a poem is also like a neutrino or dimensionless point, dressed in virtual particles, existing here and there at the same time, operating outside of ordinary reality in its own indeterminate quantum existence.

In "The Ether" (2011), Armantrout refers to how spacetime operates

104 | THE IMAGINARY PRESENT

in quantum theory. "Ether," she says, is "somewhere near / the Planck length," referencing the limit point in quantum physics, an infinitesimal dimension where the laws of physics break down.[17] She begins the poem with a comparison of classical mechanics to quantum theory: "We're out past the end / game where things get fuzzy, // less thingy, / though in past times / we practiced // precision / concrete as a slot machine." She's comparing the fuzziness or ambiguities in quantum physics to the precision of classical mechanics, which describes natural laws based on observation.

In this poem as in others, Armantrout uses poetic form to its maximum potential. The short lines and section breaks physically compress complex ideas into a minimalist body, creating a physical shorthand, a wormhole, a spatiotemporal passage for the reader to travel. Armantrout's poems do not merely explore concepts in physics at the scale of theme. Through their poetic form—their line length, line breaks, section breaks, juxtapositions, and italic emphases—they materially interact with spacetime, which warps matter while being warped by matter in turn. Armantrout's poems are hyperdimensional objects of language in the material universe, physical expressions of dimensions beyond the four of spacetime that we ordinarily experience. In their subatomic density they contain Walt Whitman's multitudes. They are tesseracts like Doctor Who's Tardis time machine, bigger on the inside than the outside.

The Matrix

Matrix mechanics, one of the two mathematics in quantum theory that Werner Heisenberg developed, challenged assumptions that the sub-atomic world mirrors the cosmological world. In contrast to notions that electrons in atoms move in orbits like planets, matrix mechanics describes the motion of electrons as jumps or leaps from one quantum state to another, suggestive of Epicurus's notion of clinamen, the atomic swerve. This conjures the possibility that clinamen is a physical force in nature like electromagnetism or gravity that exists not only in conceptual but material reality.

Conventional notions of meaning are often dependent on outdated, linear notions of time separated from space, as meaning is arrived at, in time, after comprehension or examined experience. Reading in English relies on linear ideas of time and space since grammar follows a horizontal progression from left to right that occurs before comprehension or examined experience is reached. However, the literary artform of poetry, by using the curvature of spacetime as a literary device, can subvert a reader's conventional experience with spacetime.

In a presentation by Lisa Randall at the University of Colorado Boulder, she discussed how, in the context of superstring theory, some dimensions in the theorized multiverse are called "branes," short for membranes.[1] In one superstring theory, known as membrane theory or M-Theory, there are eleven dimensions of spacetime. After her talk, I thought about literary dimensions in relation to the concept of dimensionality in physics, the homophone brain/brane, and Heisenberg's concern that ordinary language cannot adequately describe quantum theory.

Quantum poetics investigates how the creative dimensions of material reality as expressed in poetry are not as distinct from physics as convention would have us assume. Poetry and quantum physics are con-

| 105

nected by imaginary solutions within the *Imaginary Present*. In quantum poetics, the exploratory exchange between physics and poetry is not strictly science, and not strictly art, but a dialogue, which requires translation between the two fields.

There is a popular attitude among poets that the best translators of poetry from one language to another must be poets themselves, since those who write poetry can represent challenging concepts using approaches from poetry that only a poet would know. Translation in literature is also a political and historical discourse with its focus on expanding understanding between cultures. Since there is so much variation among cultures and historical periods, translating poetry between languages relies on expertise not only with poetic language but with how each culture has shaped it. The translation of a poem is always a new poem.

The usual risk of translating poetry from one language to another is that translation almost always fails at communicating what is being translated with complete accuracy. However, thinking of translation in terms of exact laws, as success and failure, does not consider that language operates within gradations of meaning. Translation in poetry is always a creative act, since the interplay of words, the experience of rhythm, and the nuances of poetic form are specific to the original language in which a poem is written. Translation evokes more questions than it can resolve, questions that imagine solutions that ask more questions.

The Explorer in Alfred Jarry's (space)time machine that forges the *Imaginary Present* by traveling to the future—and in doing so creating a second past that contains the future on their way back to the "real" present—produces imaginary solutions for the questions of the "real" present within a spacetime that is curved. This (space)time travel gives the Explorer greater artistic, rational, and poethical agency within spacetime, allowing them to intervene in two presents and their shared history, as well as the future, by influencing the now-here.

Consider that Neo, by waking up in a future where his past was a computer program that he dreamt, changes catastrophes and fortunes in the two simultaneous presents in which he lives, the "real" present of Zion and the *Imaginary Present* of *The Matrix*, both equally real and unreal in their poetic contradiction, just as the photon, a quantum particle of light, is both a wave and a particle in quantum physics.[2] In quantum poetics, which is a translation between poetry and physics, 'pataphysics is a physics of poetry and a poetics of physics. Therefore, *indefinitely*:

Poetry is the tangential point—between Brane and Brain—

Notes

Time Is Not an Arrow

1. Shing-Tung Yau and Steve Nadis, *The Shape of Inner Space: String Theory and the Geometry of the Universe's Hidden Dimensions* (New York: Basic Books, 2012), 7.

2. Charlie Wood, "Physicists Create Elusive Particles That Remember Their Pasts," *Quanta Magazine*, May 2023.

3. Werner Heisenberg, *Physics and Philosophy: The Revolution in Modern Science* (New York: Harper and Row, 1958), 147–148, 180–181.

4. Heisenberg, *Physics and Philosophy*, 58.

5. Alfred Jarry, *Selected Works of Alfred Jarry*, ed. Roger Shattuck and Simon Watson Taylor (New York: Grove Press, 1965), 121.

Writing the Speed of Light

1. Lyn Hejinian, *Happily* (Berkeley: The Post-Apollo Press, 2000), 1; Lyn Hejinian, *The Fatalist* (Richmond, CA: Omnidawn Books, 2003), 75.

2. Terence McKenna, *Alien Dreamtime*, multimedia live recording, Transmission Theater (San Francisco: 1993).

3. Leonard Shlain, *Art & Physics: Parallel Visions in Space, Time, and Light* (New York: Harper Perennial, 2001), 30–36.

4. Shlain, *Art & Physics*, 30–36.

5. Shlain, *Art & Physics*, 56, 187–192.

6. Shlain, *Art & Physics*, 188–191

7. Michio Kaku, *Physics of the Impossible* (New York: Anchor, 2009), 232.

8. Shlain, *Art & Physics*, 188–191.

9. Shlain, *Art & Physics*, 189.

10. Shlain, *Art & Physics*, 188–191.

110 | *Notes to Pages 18–28*

The Multiverse

1. Gertrude Stein, *Selected Writings of Gertrude Stein*, ed. Carl Van Vechten (New York: Vintage Books, 1990), 333.
2. Shlain, *Art & Physics*, 328–329.
3. Jim Baggott, *Beyond Measure: Modern Physics, Philosophy, and the Meaning of Quantum Theory* (Oxford: Oxford University Press, 2004), 284.
4. Lisa Randall, "Warped Passages: Unraveling the Mysteries of the Universe's Hidden Dimensions," 42nd George Gamow Memorial Lecture, University of Colorado Boulder, March 19, 2007.

The New Spacetime

1. Heisenberg, *Physics and Philosophy*, 183–184.
2. Heisenberg, *Physics and Philosophy*, 181–186.

'Pataphysics Is an Iridescent Veil

1. Alfred Jarry, *Exploits and Opinions of Doctor Faustroll, Pataphysician*, trans. Simon Watson Taylor (Cambridge, MA: Exact Change, 1996), 21, 22.
2. Roger Shattuck, *The Banquet Years: The Origins of the Avant-Garde in France 1885 to World War I*, revised edition (London: Vintage Books, 1968), 207.
3. Guillaume Apollinaire, *The Cubist Painters: Aesthetic Meditations* (New York: George Wittenborn, 1949), 13–14, quoted in Linda Dalrymple Henderson, "A New Facet of Cubism: 'The Fourth Dimension and Non-Euclidean Geometry' Reinterpreted," *Art Quarterly 34* (1971).
4. Lucretius, *The Nature of Things*, trans. Frank O. Copley (New York: W. W. Norton, 1977), 34.
5. Jarry, *Exploits and Opinions of Doctor Faustroll*, xviii.
6. Harold Bloom, *The Anxiety of Influence*, second edition (Oxford: Oxford University Press, 1997), 42.
7. Joan Retallack, *The Poethical Wager* (Berkeley: University of California Press, 2003), I.
8. Jarry, *Exploits and Opinions of Doctor Faustroll*, 88.
9. Jarry, *Exploits and Opinions of Doctor Faustroll*, 88, 89.
10. Jarry, *Exploits and Opinions of Doctor Faustroll*, 91.
11. Shattuck, *The Banquet Years*, 59–71.
12. Katie L. Price, "A ≠ A: The Potential for a 'Pataphysical Poetic in Dan Farrell's *The Inkblot Record*," *Canadian Literature* 210/211 (Autumn/Winter 2011): 27–41.
13. Stein, *Selected Writings of Gertrude Stein*, 518.

Notes to Pages 28–38 | 111

14. Jarry, *Selected Works of Alfred Jarry*, 121.

15. Gino Segrè, *Faust in Copenhagen: A Struggle for the Soul of Physics* (New York: Penguin, 2007), 133.

16. Segrè, *Faust in Copenhagen*, 134, 135.

17. Segrè, *Faust in Copenhagen*, 150, 151.

18. George Gamow, *Thirty Years That Shook Physics* (New York: Dover, 1985), 103.

19. Heisenberg, *Physics and Philosophy*, 58.

Third Mind

1. Galileo Galilei, *Dialogue Concerning the Two Chief World Systems*, trans. Stillman Drake, second revised edition (Berkeley: University of California Press, 1967), i–xix.

2. Heisenberg, *Physics and Philosophy*, 181–186.

3. Heisenberg, *Physics and Philosophy*, 183–184.

4. Werner Heisenberg, *The Physical Principles of the Quantum Theory*, trans. Carl Eckart and Frank C. Hoyt (New York: Dover, 1949), 2.

5. Heisenberg, *Physics and Philosophy*, 175.

6. Heisenberg, *The Physical Principles of the Quantum Theory*, 62–63.

The Imaginary Present

1. Alfred Jarry, *The Supermale*, trans. Ralph Gladstone and Barbara Wright (Cambridge, MA: Exact Change, 1999), 141.

2. Jarry, *The Supermale*, 93.

3. Jarry, *The Supermale*, 93–94.

4. Jarry, *The Supermale*, 95.

5. Jarry, *Exploits and Opinions of Doctor Faustroll*, 21.

6. Jarry, *Exploits and Opinions of Doctor Faustroll*, 21–22.

7. Heisenberg, *The Physical Principles of the Quantum Theory*, 62–63.

8. Jarry, *The Supermale*, 34.

9. Jarry, *The Supermale*, 34.

10. Heisenberg, *The Physical Principles of the Quantum Theory*, 20.

The Reader as a Quantum Observer

1. Lyn Hejinian, "The Rejection of Closure," in *The Language of Inquiry* (Berkeley: University of California Press, 2000), 40–82.

112 | *Notes to Pages 39–55*

Physics of the Impossible

1. M. NourbeSe Philip, *Zong!* (Middletown, CT: Wesleyan University Press, 2008), 189–206.
2. Kaku, *Physics of the Impossible*, 200.
3. M. NourbeSe Philip, conversation with author.
4. Kaku, *Physics of the Impossible*, 203.

The Poetry Accelerator

1. Christian Bök, conversation with author.
2. Bernard Carr, *Universe or Multiverse* (Cambridge, UK: Cambridge University Press, 2007), 13.

Just Schrödinger the Text!

1. Heisenberg, *Physics and Philosophy*, 45, 50, 54.
2. Daniel Kim-Shapiro, conversation with author.
3. Heisenberg, *The Physical Principles of the Quantum Theory*, 64.
4. Heisenberg, *The Physical Principles of the Quantum Theory*, 64.
5. Segrè, *Faust in Copenhagen*, 141–148.
6. Segrè, *Faust in Copenhagen*, 141–148.
7. Segrè, *Faust in Copenhagen*, 141–148.
8. Segrè, *Faust in Copenhagen*, 141–148.
9. Segrè, *Faust in Copenhagen*, 143.
10. Segrè, *Faust in Copenhagen*, 142.
11. Segrè, *Faust in Copenhagen*, 148–153.

Spin the Kaleidoscope

1. National Radio Astronomy Observatory, "Huge Superbubble of Gas Blowing Out of Milky Way," news release, January 12, 2006, <https://public .nrao.edu/news/huge-superbubble-of-gas-blowing-out-of-milky-way/>.
2. *The Telepathic Motion Picture of THE LOST TRIBES*, directed by David Blair (1994–present); *Wax or the Discovery of Television Among the Bees*, directed by David Blair (1991); WAXWEB (1994), directed by David Blair (1993), <http://waxweb.org>.

Notes to Pages 56–73 | 113

Poetry and the Fourth Dimension

1. Shanxing Wang, *Mad Science in Imperial City* (New York: Futurepoem Books, 2005), 80.
2. *The Diary of Virginia Woolf*, vol. 3, ed. Anne Olivier Bell (New York: Mariner Books, 1981), Saturday, June 18, 1927, 139.

The People of the Fifth Dimension

1. Charles Stein, conversations with author.
2. Stein, conversations.
3. Stein, conversations.

The Positron Passport

1. Heisenberg, *Physics and Philosophy*, 177–179.
2. Heisenberg, *Physics and Philosophy*, 176.
3. Heisenberg, *Physics and Philosophy*, 177.
4. Heisenberg, *Physics and Philosophy*, 58.
5. Emily Dickinson, *The Complete Poems of Emily Dickinson*, ed. Thomas H. Johnson, eleventh edition (Boston: Little, Brown, 1960), 448.
6. Lucretius, *The Nature of Things*, 31.
7. Gian Giudice, conversation with author; Gian Giudice, "Why Our Universe Might Exist on a Knife-Edge."
8. Giudice, conversations with author.
9. Giudice, conversations with author; Roberto Franceschini, Gian F. Giudice, Jernej F. Kamenik, Matthew McCullough, Riva Francesco, Alessandro Strumi, Riccardo Torre, "Digamma: What Next?," Report no. CERN-TH-2016–090, May 11, 2016, 3, <https://arxiv.org/pdf/1604.06446.pdf>.
10. Sarah Kaplan "Speaking of Science," *Washington Post*, December 20, 2016, <https://www.washingtonpost.com/news/speaking-of-science/wp/20 16/12/20/in-breakthrough-experiment-scientists-shine-a-light-on-antimat ter/?utm_term=.7ac1f6302b91>.
11. Gamow, *Thirty Years That Shook Physics*, 165.
12. Gamow, *Thirty Years That Shook Physics*, 168; Segrè, *Faust in Copenhagen*, 47.
13. Gamow, *Thirty Years That Shook Physics*, 168.
14. Gamow, *Thirty Years That Shook Physics*, 205.
15. Gamow, *Thirty Years That Shook Physics*, 205–6.
16. Luis Álvarez-Gaumé, conversation with author, CERN.
17. David Blair, conversations with author, text and email.

114 | *Notes to Pages 73–83*

18. Juan José Gómez Cadenas, conversations with author, email.

19. Gómez Cadenas, conversations with author.

20. Gómez Cadenas, conversations with author.

21. Rainer Marie Rilke, "The Unicorn," trans., William Pratt, *The Sewanee Review* (1966): 807.

22. Heisenberg, *Physics and Philosophy*, 185.

23. American Institute of Physics, "Oral History Interviews: Werner Heisenberg," interview by Joan Bromberg, June 16, 1970, <https://www.aip.org/history-programs/niels-bohr-library/oral-histories/5027>.

24. Heisenberg, *The Physical Principles of the Quantum Theory*, 10.

25. Bashō, *The Essential Haiku: Versions of Bashō, Buson, and Issa*, trans. Robert Hass (Hopewell, NJ: The Ecco Press, 1994), 18.

26. Mina Loy, *The Lost Lunar Baedeker: Poems of Mina Loy*, ed. Roger L. Conover (New York: Farrar, Straus and Giroux, 1997), 1.

27. Dōgen, *Moon In a Dewdrop: Writings of Zen Master Dōgen*, ed. Kazuaki Tanashi, trans. Robert Aitken et al. (Berkeley, CA: North Point Press, 1985).

28. Heisenberg, *The Physical Principles of the Quantum Theory*, 3.

29. Heisenberg, *The Physical Principles of the Quantum Theory*, 64.

30. Will Alexander, *Towards the Primeval Lightning Field* (Oakland: O Books, 1998), 100.

31. "Recommendations on the Immediate Use of Nuclear Weapons, by the Scientific Panel of the Interim Committee on Nuclear Power, June 16, 1945," <http://www.dannen.com/decision/scipanel.html>; Atomic Heritage Foundation, "Enrico Fermi," accessed July 30, 2017, <http://www.atomicheritage.org/profile/enrico-fermi>.

32. Bern Porter, *Sounds That Arouse Me: Selected Writings of Bern Porter*, ed. Mark Melnicove (Gardiner, ME: Tilbury House, 1993), i-ii.

33. Porter, *Sounds That Arouse Me*, ii.

34. Mark Melnicove, conversation with author, email.

35. Porter, *Sounds That Arouse Me*, 127.

36. Porter, *Sounds That Arouse Me*, 127.

37. Niayesh Afshordi, Robert B. Mann, and Razieh Pourhasan, *Scientific American* 24, no. 4 (Winter 2015): 6.

To Be in Any Form

1. Walt Whitman, *Leaves of Grass*, Modern Library Edition (New York: Random House, 1993), 71.

2. Whitman, *Leaves of Grass*, 71.

The Password to the Quantum Supercomputer Poem Will Be NCC-1701

1. Henry David Thoreau, *Walden* (The Project Gutenberg eBook of Walden, 1995), ebook.
2. *Star Trek*, directed by J. J. Abrams (Hollywood: Paramount Pictures, 2009).
3. Essays of Ralph Waldo Emerson, "Nature" (New York: Literary Classics, Inc., 1945) 256.
4. *Mill Valley Record*, no. 24, August 12, 1922.

The Violet Doorway

1. mIEKAL aND, *Samsara Congeries* (Buffalo, NY: BlazeVox Books, 2016).
2. aND, *Samsara Congeries*, 3, 4, 57, 493.
3. aND, *Samsara Congeries*, 80.
4. aND, *Samsara Congeries*, 101, 106.
5. aND, *Samsara Congeries*, 122.
6. aND, *Samsara Congeries*, 302, 313.
7. aND, *Samsara Congeries*, 353, 360.
8. aND, *Samsara Congeries*, 364.
9. aND, *Samsara Congeries*, 377.
10. aND, *Samsara Congeries*, 408, 419, 433, 437.
11. aND, *Samsara Congeries*, 503.
12. aND, *Samsara Congeries*, 513.
13. aND, *Samsara Congeries*, 514.

Poetry in Superposition

1. James Joyce, *Finnegans Wake* (London: Faber and Faber, 1975), 4.
2. Lucretius, *The Nature of Things*.
3. Jarry, *Exploits and Opinions of Doctor Faustroll*, 91.

U+F+O+L+A+N+G+U+A+G+E

1. Christine Wertheim, *mUtter-bAbel* (Denver, CO: Counterpath Books, 2013).
2. Derek Beaulieu, *Please: No More Poetry: The Poetry of derek beaulieu* (Ontario: Wilfrid Laurier University Press, 2013), 23–28.

116 | *Notes to Pages 92–99*

3. Craig Dworkin and Kenneth Goldsmith, eds., *Against Expression, An Anthology of Conceptual Writing* (Evanston, IL: Northwestern University Press, 2011), 64–72.

4. Jennifer K. Dick, "CERN 43," *Cordite Poetry Review*, February 1, 2014, <http://cordite.org.au/chapbooks-features/spoonbending/cern-43/>.

The Subtle Web of Thought

1. American Institute of Physics, "Oral History Interviews: Werner Heisenberg."

2. Heisenberg, *Physics and Philosophy*, 167, 168, 174, 177.

3. Heisenberg, *Physics and Philosophy*, 171.

4. Heisenberg, *Physics and Philosophy*, 171.

5. kevin mcpherson eckhoff, *rhapsodomancy*, 81

6. Hejinian, *The Language of Inquiry*, 40–58.

7. Hejinian, *The Language of Inquiry*, 42–43.

8. Hejinian, *The Language of Inquiry*, 43.

9. Hejinian, *The Language of Inquiry*, 42.

Metaphor and Decay

1. Heisenberg, *Physics and Philosophy*, 54.

2. Whitman, *Leaves of Grass*, 40.

The Origami Time Machine

1. Grant Morrison, *The Invisibles* (New York: Vertigo/DC Comics, 1994–2000), vol. 5, 49.

2. Morrison, *The Invisibles*, vol. 5, 51.

The Physics of Existence

1. Rae Armantrout, *Veil: New and Selected* (Middletown, CT: Wesleyan University Press, 2001), 43.

2. Rae Armantrout, *Itself* (Middletown, CT: Wesleyan University Press, 2015), 3.

3. Armantrout, *Itself*, 3.

4. Armantrout, *Itself*, 3.

Notes to Pages 100–7 | 117

5. Rae Armantrout, *Just Saying* (Middletown, CT: Wesleyan University Press, 2013), 6.

6. Armantrout, *Just Saying*, 7.

7. Armantrout, *Itself*, 20.

8. Armantrout, *Itself*, 20.

9. Armantrout, *Itself*, 20.

10. Rae Armantrout, *Versed* (Middletown, CT: Wesleyan University Press, 2009), 85.

11. Armantrout, *Versed*, 85.

12. Armantrout, *Versed*, 85.

13. Armantrout, *Versed*, 148.

14. Armantrout, *Versed*, 148.

15. Rae Armantrout, *Money Shot* (Middletown, CT: Wesleyan University Press, 2012), 37.

16. Heisenberg, *Physics and Philosophy*, 58.

17. Armantrout, *Money Shot*, 37.

The Matrix

1. Randall, "Warped Passages."

2. *The Matrix*, directed by Lilly Wachowski and Lana Wachowski (Burbank, CA: Warner Bros., 1999); *The Matrix Reloaded*, directed by Lilly Wachowski and Lana Wachowski (Burbank, CA: Warner Bros. Pictures, 2003); *The Matrix Revolutions*, directed by Lilly Wachowski and Lana Wachowski (Burbank, CA: Warner Bros., 2003); *The Matrix Resurrections*, directed by Lana Wachowski (Burbank, CA: Warner Bros. Pictures, 2023).